Get Into Classical Music

Get Into Classical Music

Chris Craker

BANTAM BOOKS
TORONTO • NEW YORK • LONDON • SYDNEY • AUCKLAND

GET INTO CLASSICAL MUSIC
Based on an original concept by
Chris Craker and Mark Chapple

A BANTAM BOOK 0 553 40440 7

First publication in Great Britain

PRINTING HISTORY
Bantam edition published 1991
Bantam edition reprinted 1992 (twice)

This book is set in 11/12pt Plantin by
Kestrel Data, Exeter

Bantam Books are published by Transworld Publishers Ltd., 61–63 Uxbridge Road, Ealing, London W5 5SA, in Australia by Transworld Publishers (Australia) Pty. Ltd., 15–23 Helles Avenue, Moorebank, NSW 2170, and in New Zealand by Transworld Publishers (N.Z.) Ltd., 3 William Pickering Drive, Albany, Auckland.

Printed and bound in Great Britain by
Cox & Wyman Ltd., Reading, Berks.

Contents

Author's Note and Acknowledgements

Countless people have come to me after concerts and delivered the immortal line 'I do love classical music – I don't know much about it – but I know what I like when I hear it.' This book is for you.

My thanks go first to Mark Chapple, who sowed the seed for the idea and whose commitment to the whole project is greatly appreciated. My thanks also to Kate (for unfailing support and encouragement), Jane Jones and finally, Klaus Heymann of Naxos.

Chris Craker
June 1991

Preface

The year 1990 will go down in history as being one of the most significant in the wider appreciation of classical music. It was the year when, owing to the impact made by just a couple of fine musicians, classical music found a place in the hearts of millions of people all over the world.

I am, of course, referring to the activities of the violinist Nigel Kennedy and the singer Luciano Pavarotti who, in conjunction with their record companies and marketing men, have played a major role in making classical music accessible to a much wider audience than ever before. Pavarotti's superb rendition of Puccini's '*Nessun dorma*', used as the BBC's theme tune for the television coverage of the World Cup from Italy, is the obvious case in point. This was followed by the enormously successful concert given by the 'Three Tenors' (Pavarotti joined by Placido Domingo and José Carreras) broadcast live from Rome to the largest-ever audience for a classical music event. This historic concert is naturally available on CD, record and cassette and ranks alongside Nigel Kennedy's recording of Vivaldi's *The Four Seasons* as being one of the most successful classical releases of all time.

So what happened? This music has been around for centuries and talented musicians have been tirelessly playing it in concert halls all around the world. There are recordings available in specialist record shops, department stores, petrol stations and now even in supermarkets. You need only switch on the radio or television to be able to listen to the world's finest artists performing great music. Yet until quite recently the general public has seen classical music as very much a minority interest and as an art form about which one should really have 'specialist' knowledge.

This state of affairs has arisen for a number of reasons, perhaps the main one being the idea that going to classical music concerts is rather an upper-class or élitist thing to do. This is obviously ridiculous. Classical music can be enjoyed by anyone. To put this into perspective, remember that, although commissioned to write music by the aristocracy of the day, Mozart and Haydn were writing to entertain and provide musical satisfaction for people from all walks of life – from kings and queens right down to the servants and members of the general public. This was the popular music of the time. If Mozart had been around today, he would have held cult status as the most celebrated of pop stars.

One reason why the 'élitist' label attaches itself to classical music in the twentieth century is the fact that musicians have been a little guilty of presenting themselves rather formally for many years now, both in the way that they dress and the 'barriers' that have been created between the performer and the audience in the concert hall. But now, solo artists like Nigel Kennedy and orchestras like the LCO (London Chamber Orchestra) are making the first real efforts to dress in a contemporary style. By and large this has been very successful – although there was a case towards the end of 1990 when Nigel Kennedy painted his face white, with drips of stage blood, for a performance of the Berg *Violin Concerto*. Popular opinion suggests that this episode took the point a bit too far.

Many people I talk to bring up the 'code of conduct' that should be adhered to in concerts, whereby people are afraid of clapping in the wrong place and are nervous of coughing in the quiet moments. More and more, however, it's becoming common for the performers to introduce the pieces and attempt to put the audience at ease. This need not detract from the 'atmosphere-creating' process and can indeed enhance it when done well. Research suggests that the vast majority of people in the audience prefer to have a more direct contact with the performers. Some orchestras are even taking this a stage further, by arranging for drinks receptions after the concert at which the audience can mingle with and talk to the performers – a move that seems to have been welcomed.

So things are changing. Owing to the efforts of artists like Nigel Kennedy, Pavarotti, Dudley Moore, James Galway and the LCO, millions of people from all age-groups, cultures and backgrounds have been made aware of some of the finest music written in the last few centuries, simply because it's been presented in a way that is appealing and relevant to today's audience. The surprising fact is that this is music to which, a couple of years ago, most people would probably have never given a second thought, let alone a second hearing. But now they have become familiar with pieces by Puccini, Vivaldi, Ravel and many others. They no longer feel embarrassed about admitting that they like them and the CDs, records and cassettes can sit proudly on their shelves alongside those by Dire Straits, Pink Floyd, the Pet Shop Boys and Richard Clayderman.

Where do we go from here? If you are one of the people who has recently become aware of classical music and want to know more, or you fall into the category of people who 'know what they like when they hear it', then this is the book for you. Possibly you heard the music in the Hamlet cigar commercial and rather liked it; or perhaps you felt shivers go down your spine when the wonderfully romantic music in the film *Brief Encounter* was playing. The fact is that there's a whole world of music, waiting to be discovered and with the aid of *Get Into Classical Music* you are the one who is going to discover it.

Good record shops have daunting rows of CDs, records and cassettes. How do you know which of the dozens of versions of each piece to choose? What's the difference between a symphony and a concerto? Would you know how to distinguish between a sonata and an overture? Does it even matter? *Get Into Classical Music* is the no-nonsense guide that will answer all these questions and more. It will give you an introduction to the finest classical music and will point you in the right direction, enabling you to become familiar with and hopefully enjoy, all styles of classical music. In addition, you can find out which music has been made famous on television, in films and commercials and also learn a little about the instruments involved, as well as the inside story on the composers.

At the end of each section on the 'Top Fifty Composers' there is a list of pieces that are really essential listening. These come under the heading of 'Recommended Listening'. If you like what you've heard, then go on to 'Further Listening', which is a list of works by the same composer, not necessarily his most famous pieces but those that are definitely worth investigation. At the end of each group of composers (the Baroque, the Classical, the Romantics, and so on) there's a 'Where to Go from Here' section that guides you to the works of the lesser known composers who wrote in a similar style.

Introduction
Your Starter Top Ten

The aim of this book is to introduce you to classical music in a 'user-friendly' way, avoiding excessive use of technical jargon and providing an interesting and stimulating way forward in your search for good classical music that you will enjoy.

Let me start by being completely honest with you. Not all classical music is user-friendly and accessible. Even music by some of the famous household names can be difficult and require more than a casual listening, in order really to get to grips with it. With this in mind, let's start off with some music that you are almost certain to enjoy and appreciate: ten pieces I can guarantee – well, *almost* guarantee! – that you will find immediately appealing. These are, of course, my personal choices and there's bound to be some disagreement between us, which is good because it means you may have already developed your own favourites. Here they are then – my personal recommendations to you. They are all to be found on *Get Into Classical Music Volume 1*, advertised at the end of the book and available in selected record and book shops, although there are literally dozens of versions available on separate albums that you can find at most good record shops, should you wish to buy them individually. *Get Into Classical Music Volume 1* also includes other works that are mentioned in the course of the book and acquiring this recording may well be the most cost-effective and efficient way to get to know the pieces in question.

As you'll see throughout the book, classical music falls into a number of well-defined categories – mostly either by period (as in the Baroque, the Classical and the

Romantic) or by groups or schools of composers (as in the Impressionists and the Nationalists). These periods and schools of composers are all dealt with in more detail later, but at this stage there is no earthly reason why you *need* to know anything very much about them at all. Just sit back and listen. I hope that you will find, however, that you really do get more out of it all when you know the background; but for now just enjoy the music and remember that you are listening to what was essentially the pop music of the day. The notion that classical music should be listened to in complete silence and with almost spiritual reverence is one that has been cultivated by those wishing to impress us. Up until the nineteenth century concerts were invariably boozy occasions at which people chatted, danced and sang along to the music. Arias (songs) from Mozart's operas were sung in the beer-houses in Vienna by the lager louts of the day and you would probably have found it hard to resist tapping your foot or dancing to the music of Handel or Vivaldi.

In this 'starter list' I've chosen examples from each of the most important and popular types of classical music. You will not be disappointed and you may already know one or two of the pieces that have been made famous in films or in television commercials.

Your Starter Top Ten

VIVALDI:
Third movement, '*Autumn*', from *The Four Seasons* (Baroque)
HANDEL:
'*The Arrival of the Queen of Sheba*' (Baroque)
MOZART:
Rondo from *Eine Kleine Nachtmusik* (Classical)
BEETHOVEN:
Adagio from the '*Moonlight*' *Sonata* (Classical)
MENDELSSOHN:
Scherzo from *A Midsummer Night's Dream* (Classical)

CHOPIN:
Fantasie Impromptu (Romantic)
RACHMANINOV:
First movement, Piano Concerto No. 2 (Romantic)
DEBUSSY:
Clair de lune (Impressionistic)
GERSHWIN:
Rhapsody in Blue (American)
PUCCINI:
'*Nessun dorma*' (Romantic, Italian, Opera)

These pieces, which I describe in detail later, give a great introduction to many of the different types of classical music mentioned in the book; and, in just the same way that not all of us really appreciate heavy metal or soul music, many will find that they prefer Debussy to Vivaldi. The only way to find out is to make yourself familiar with the music in question. With the aid of this book and the recording your task should be that much easier.

I shall never forget the enjoyment and satisfaction derived from 'discovering' a new pop album as a teenager and this applies in just the same way to discovering the joys of classical music. *Get Into Classical Music* will open new doors for you while giving you some useful information along the way in an approachable and easy-going manner. I cannot overstress the importance of being adventurous in your quest for finding music that you will like. Try to make the effort to go and hear a live concert or two. There's an incredible choice of concerts every week all over the country and once you have done a little bit of homework and background reading (so that you know what you are in for) making the effort to go along and experience some classical music first-hand will, I am sure, be thoroughly enjoyable.

Dip into the book wherever takes your fancy. You don't have to read it in any particular order, although it might be useful to know that the first chapter may provide some answers to questions you have about technical terms. The main part of the book is set out in a fairly chronological way; but if you feel moved to read about Mahler before Mozart, then do as you please. There are no rules here.

I hope that you enjoy the book and that it will open up a world of music that will provide entertainment for you, your family and friends for many years to come. Forget all the stigmas, read the book, switch on the tape, sit back, relax and, above all, enjoy the music!

List of Abbreviations

Each work mentioned in the listening-lists is accompanied by one of the following abbreviations to indicate what type of work it is.

Ch = chamber
I = instrumental
O = orchestral
Op = opera
Or = oratorio
Org = organ music
V = vocal

Chapter One

What Exactly Is Classical Music?

To the majority of people the term 'classical music' seems to be the one used to describe almost any music that is played by orchestras and musicians wearing white tie and tails, or any other 'serious' music that doesn't automatically fall into the specific categories of pop, rock, jazz, ethnic or new age. However, this is not strictly the case. To be really pedantic, 'classical music' is the music that was written from around the mid-eighteenth century through to the early part of the nineteenth century, encompassing the works of composers like Mozart and Beethoven.

At the time when Bach, Mozart and Beethoven were writing, their music was the popular music of the day; but it has now been dubbed 'classical', playing on the exact dictionary definition of the word meaning simple, harmonious and formally structured. This umbrella title encompasses many different styles: Baroque, Romantic, Impressionistic and Nationalistic schools are just a few examples. Pop music suffers the same fate: the title 'pop music' has to cover a multitude of styles – from soul to reggae and from heavy metal to hip-hop.

Confusing though it is, do remember that the term 'classical music' can either be applied to the music specifically written between the years 1750 and 1827 or be used as the all-encompassing title for serious music – or not so serious, as we may well find out.

Where did it all start? Man's empathy and feeling for music is an absolutely fundamental part of our being and there is much evidence to support the belief that, from the beginning, primitive man experimented with both rhythm and melody by beating different-sized sticks of wood and stretching skin over scooped-out logs to make the earliest form of drums. As time went by, the instruments became more and more sophisticated and man's perception of what was 'musical' developed accordingly. During the course of this book we're going to look at the main styles of music that have achieved mass appeal since about 1685 (the start of the Baroque era). There are, of course, many devotees of medieval music and the early sacred music, much of which was written in Italy by composers like Monteverdi, Palestrina and others, but for our purposes we are going to concentrate on classical music from 1685. If you feel drawn to the early forms of music, I suggest a closer study may well be beneficial.

Nor are we going to have a detailed look at the music of today since I feel that the main purpose of this book is to get you to feel comfortable with music that has been 'tried and tested' by audiences around the world for some time. Once you have built up your confidence with the music of the masters and have ascertained where your general taste and preference lies, then you may well have a lot of fun in exploring the works of some of today's composers. Take a look at the chapter entitled 'Where Next?' for a few helpful guidelines; and, if you do decide to go down any of these routes, try to make the effort to go and hear the works performed live in the concert hall. Somehow seeing the musicians hard at work adds to the enjoyment of the whole experience.

A short explanation follows on the sorts of technical terms and phrases that you will come across in the book, in record-sleeve notes or in concert programmes. You may have heard a lot of them before but, so that you know exactly what is being referred to, I've tried to cover all the main expressions that are mentioned.

THE PERFORMERS

Orchestra

Orchestras come in four basic types: the standard symphony orchestra (comprising large forces of strings, wind instruments, a brass section and percussion), the chamber orchestra (a scaled-down version of the above), the original-instrument orchestra (using instruments of the period in which the composer was writing and the exact number envisaged by that composer) and the string orchestra (consisting of violins, violas, cellos and double basses).

The orchestra has developed throughout the centuries, usually by increasing the number of players and the term can also be applied to a large body of wind and brass instruments – the wind orchestra, which some would malign as being a glorified military band!

For a perfect example of all the divisions of the orchestra playing both separately and together, do make a point of listening to Benjamin Britten's *Young Person's Guide to the Orchestra*. It is a marvellous work in its own right and you don't have to be young to enjoy it.

Conductor

Originally, the job of the present-day conductor was undertaken by either the leader of the orchestra (the principal violinist) or the harpsichordist. Concertos were conducted by the soloist in close liaison with the leader and there was never a need for an independent person to wave the baton.

However, as music became more complex it was

necessary for someone to take control of the proceedings and direct both the rehearsals and the concert performance. There are more than a few orchestral players who might now try to persuade you that the role of the conductor was created when musicians spotted an opportunity of receiving higher fees and taking all the glory while not even having to play a single note, but there is only a small grain of truth in this!

The conductor of an orchestra has enormous power, for it is he or she who has the control of the overall shape of the piece – the speed (or tempo) at which the piece should be played and the level of sound that each section of the orchestra should perform at. More importantly the conductor is responsible for inspiring the players to give of their best. This is a rare and highly valued quality and is why top conductors receive very big fees compared to the players. As you can imagine, this is sometimes the basis for friction, but is usually kept in abeyance as conductors like to maintain as good a relationship with their players as possible.

Soloist

The soloist is the singer or instrumentalist taking the solo part in a work with orchestra. The term can sometimes also be applied to a duo; for example, where there is a violinist playing music for violin and piano, the pianist will often be labelled as the accompanist while the violinist is the soloist.

Soloists appear taking the solo part in works called concertos (see below) and are often outstandingly gifted performers. Necessary qualities include an extremely fine technique and unique creativity. They are quite often flamboyant characters and a strong personality is most definitely an advantage. Some of the famous soloists of the past few years include the singers Luciano Pavarotti, Kiri Te Kanawa, Placido Domingo and José Carreras and instrumentalists Nigel Kennedy, Vladimir Ashkenazy and James Galway.

String Quartet

The string quartet consists of four people playing two violins, a viola and a cello. It was really established as a standard combination by the eighteenth century and some of the finest works for the quartet were composed by Mozart, Haydn, Schubert and Beethoven, while more modern composers like Bartók and Shostakovich have also made exceptional contributions to the repertoire.

One of the most famous groups to have performed on a regular basis was the Amadeus String Quartet and to hear them playing Mozart's *'Hunt' Quartet, K. 458,* for example, would be a fine introduction to music of this type.

Piano Trio

Confusingly, a piano trio is not a piece for three pianos. The standard combination of a piano trio includes a violin and a cello with piano. Again Mozart, Haydn, Beethoven and Schubert were the ones who really provided the 'standard' repertoire. Other composers who have been inspired to write excellent works for this combination include Schumann, Brahms, Debussy and Ravel.

A good introduction to the music for piano trio, if you have never heard one, would be to listen to Beethoven's *'Archduke' Trio Op. 97.*

Chamber Music

Chamber music is the term given to 'serious' music for two or more players up to the size of a smallish orchestra (of about fifteen players). There are a number of standard combinations that the mainstream classical composers wrote for, two of which, the string quartet and the piano trio, are described in more detail above. The remaining combinations are: violin and piano duo, cello and piano duo, string trio (violin, viola and cello), string quintet (as string quartet with either an added viola or cello), piano quintet (string quartet and piano), string sextet (two violins, two violas and two cellos) and wind quintet (flute, oboe, clarinet, horn and bassoon). In addition to these are other more diverse combinations for which various composers felt inspired to write.

MUSICAL FORMS

Movement

A movement is the term given to the main division of a piece of music. It is a complete section that makes sense in its own right but that is most normally performed within the context of the whole piece.

Overture

There are now two types of overture: First, the sort that is meant specifically to be played at the start of an opera, oratorio or ballet and, second, the sort that is specifically written to be played on its own at the start of a regular orchestral concert. Just to confuse matters, however, it is quite common to hear overtures from operas performed out of context at the start of concerts.

In the seventeenth and eighteenth centuries an overture implied a piece in three movements: Italian overtures would be quick-slow-quick, while French overtures would be slow-quick-slow. Later in the eighteenth century it was the composer Gluck who decided that an overture should be used 'to prepare the audience for the plot of the play'. Mozart, Haydn, Beethoven and later Wagner all thought this was a good idea and that is how it remains today.

Good overtures to listen to are: Mozart's *The Marriage of Figaro*, Beethoven's *Egmont*, Mendelssohn's *Hebrides* and the *Academic Festival Overture* by Brahms.

Concerto

Usually second in a standard orchestral concert programme, a concerto is a piece for a solo instrumentalist (or a few solo instrumentalists) playing with an orchestra. In the sixteenth and early seventeenth centuries the word *concerto* merely implied a piece for lots of people playing together. By the end of the seventeenth century, however, it was generally accepted that a concerto would feature a small group of string players (the *concertante, soli* or *concertato*) playing in alternation with a larger body (the *ripieno*). The title *concerto grosso* was introduced, meaning 'great concerto', and the best examples of this type are Bach's *Brandenburg Concertos*, which feature a small group of soloists playing alongside, and in alternation with, a small orchestra.

This idea developed to the point where Haydn, Mozart and Beethoven wrote concertos purely for a single soloist with orchestra – and this was sometimes called a virtuoso concerto (a virtuoso being someone who is highly skilled in the art of performance), but it is now simply called a concerto.

Listen to Mozart's *Piano Concerto No. 21*, Mendelssohn's *Violin Concerto* and the *5th* or *'Emperor' Concerto* (for piano) by Beethoven for excellent examples.

Symphony

The word *symphony* comes from the Greek meaning 'sounding together', but like the overture and the concerto it changed its meaning as time went on. Handel put a spanner in the works when he called an instrumental piece in his oratorio *Messiah* '*The Pastoral Symphony*', when it would have made life much simpler to have just called it an overture to the second act.

Symphonies as we know them developed from the sonata form (see below), which was a basic structure for writing pieces in the seventeenth century. As a rule, a symphony would be in four movements, although there are plenty of exceptions! The usual pattern for these four movements is fast, slow, minuet, fast; but, as time went on, some composers changed this format to suit their own particular creative needs, so that the term *symphony* has been applied to almost all kinds of largish-scale orchestral works that do not feature a soloist.

Listen to Mozart's *Symphony No. 40*, Beethoven's *Symphony No. 5* or Tchaikovsky's *Symphony No. 6* for wonderful examples.

Symphonic Poem

The composer Liszt is reputed to have invented this term, otherwise known as the 'tone poem' in certain circles. Essentially a symphonic poem is a piece for orchestra that has some kind of literary, dramatic or pictorial association. It is in one continuous movement that the composer moulds into whatever form he so desires for optimum creative freedom to suit his subject-matter. Music with such a connotation can also be known as programme music.

The famous writers of symphonic poems are Liszt, Richard Strauss and Smetana, among others. Listen to *Les Préludes* by Liszt or the stunning *Till Eulenspiegel* by Richard Strauss for two classic examples, but don't forget that Vivaldi wrote *The Four Seasons* more than a hundred years earlier!

Suite

A suite is the name given to a piece consisting of a chain of dance movements. During the seventeenth and eighteenth centuries it was one of the most important forms of music and there are four types of dance which conventionally appear in suites of the Baroque era: the *allemande*, the *courante*, the *sarabande* and the *gigue*.

Interestingly these have four different countries of origin: the *allemande* from Germany, the *courante* from France (or Italy), the *sarabande* from Spain and the *gigue* from either England or Ireland.

Bach wrote a number of *French Suites* for keyboard instruments and orchestral suites utilizing the forces of a small chamber orchestra. Later examples can be found in Grieg's *Peer Gynt* and Stravinsky's *Firebird* – and these do not strictly conform to the original dance forms but are more contemporary adaptations of the same.

Minuet and Trio

The minuet and trio is another dance type of movement often inserted into later forms of the suite. The minuet originated in France and was one of the approved dances at the court of Louis XIV. It was a graceful, stately dance, but as time went on Haydn and Mozart livened the whole thing up and in the hands of Beethoven the character changed so much that he eventually replaced it with an even faster movement called the scherzo.

Minuets were expanded to contain another short section within the piece called the trio. This comes as a middle section before a repetition of the original minuet. There are lovely examples of minuet and trios in Mozart's *Eine Kleine Nachtmusik* and his *Clarinet Quintet, K. 485,* an interesting feature of the latter being that Mozart actually incorporated two trio sections within the whole movement.

Sonata

The word *sonata* literally means 'sounded' as opposed to sung. In the seventeenth and early part of the eighteenth centuries there were two varieties: the *sonata da camera* (chamber sonata) and the *sonata da chiesa* (church sonata). Both were written for string instruments with keyboard accompaniment, the difference being that the chamber type was based on a series of movements featuring dance rhythms while the church type was altogether more serious in character.

Without getting too technical, it all started to settle down at about the time of Mozart and Beethoven when the established composers decided on a four-movement work rather like the symphony: fast, slow, minuet or scherzo and finally a fast finale-type movement. Unlike symphonies, however, a sonata is usually played by one or two players. Try Schubert's *Violin Sonata in A major* or the *Piano Sonata in C, K. 330*, by Mozart for perfect examples of the form.

Sonatina

A sonatina is usually either a short sonata or a lightweight, less developed piece in basically the same form.

Sonata Form

This is the term given to a basic 'blueprint' for composers to follow in order to give a structure to a single movement within a piece of their music. Later composers found this all a bit restrictive and went on to do their own thing. However, the composers in the seventeenth century were very keen on this idea and their works do more often than not stick to the rules of sonata form. The piece is split up into three basic sections: the exposition, the development and the recapitulation. As in the first part of a play we are introduced to the main characters, in the exposition we hear the main tunes, quite often two (the first and second subjects) and this section will be linked by a short bridge passage to the development section in which the composer usually winds things up emotionally and develops the tunes (often to the point where we cannot recognize them) thereby creating tension and drama. The recapitulation is where it all calms down again, often repeating a lot of the exposition with a few small changes. Quite often there is also a coda added at the end – a short passage to bring the piece to a close.

Theme and Variations

This is a form that has been commonly adopted by many composers whereby the initial theme is presented and then modified several times over, usually melodically, rhythmically or harmonically. Sometimes composers took a tune by someone else and did their own set of variations on that particular theme. For example, numerous composers have been inspired to write variations on Paganini's *24th Caprice*, ranging from Rachmaninov to Andrew Lloyd Webber (whose composition has subsequently been used as the signature tune to LWT's 'South Bank Show' presented by Melvyn Bragg).

Other marvellous examples are to be found in Bach's *Goldberg Variations*, Beethoven's *Diabelli Variations* (for harpsichord and piano respectively) and the *Variations on a Rococo Theme Op. 33* by Tchaikovsky (for cello and orchestra).

The Music Itself

Melody

This, of course, is another name for the 'tune', but in some circles can also be called a 'subject'; hence the first tune in a piece of music may also be referred to as the 'first subject' and so on.

Key

You will hear this word mentioned a lot, as most music written between the fifteenth century and the middle of the twentieth century is referred to as being 'in the key of . . .' This really means that the piece is based on the notes of a particular major or minor scale with the first note in such a scale giving its letter-name to the key in question.

Scale

The word *scale* comes from the Latin word *scala* and literally means 'a ladder'. When applied to music it is the stepwise arrangement of notes within a particular key. There are many kinds of scale, but the ones that are most commonly referred to include major scales (generally happy-sounding) and minor ones (definitely sadder and more mysterious in character). Take it from this that most pieces in a major key are generally brighter in character than those in minor keys.

Other types of scale that you may hear mentioned are 'whole-tone' and 'pentatonic' scales. These tend to be used by the modern and Impressionistic composers and have also been developed by jazz composers. They have a distinctly 'different' sound to them and you should listen to Debussy's *La fille aux cheveux de lin* for a good example of music using a pentatonic scale.

Chords

Two or more notes sounding together are known as a chord. Chords can take a number of forms. There are those which sound basically acceptable to us all (such as those found in the music of Haydn and Mozart) and these are known as diatonic. They take their form in a regular way from notes in normal scales. However, with the advent of the Romantic composers and those that followed, more and more use of unusual notes within chords was introduced to produce more emotional effects, some composers even using direct clashes of notes (discords) to create tension in their music.

Where chords move from one to another, this is called a progression and again, there are standard progressions to which we all can relate; but many composers were search- ing for new progressions to make their music sound different and consequently more interesting.

Modulation

This is another term that you may well come across within the programme notes of a standard concert and what it means is moving away from the already established key of the music. So if a piece is based in the key of A major and, halfway through, the composer subtly moves the music into F sharp minor or any other key, one would say that the music had modulated.

Dynamics and Expression Marks

Dynamics within a piece of music are the words or indications given by composers to assist the performers in playing the piece at exactly the right level of sound as the composer envisaged. There are all sorts of symbols that are used within the sheet music to denote these inflections and for a comprehensive guide to these technical terms you should consult a good dictionary of music.

Expression marks are also included within the printed music to further assist the performers in adhering to the composer's intentions. These are words giving specific guidance as to how fast or slow and in what style the music should be played. Dynamics and expression marks are usually written in Italian, but French and German composers tended to stick to their own language.

Chapter Two

Get Into Classical Music Volume 1
The Music on the CD and Cassette

The collection on the recording advertised at the end of the book represents a cross-section of pieces covering most of the styles of music mentioned in the text. It's not exhaustive – it can't be – but it does give an excellent introduction to the main popular styles of classical music as well as being a really interesting collection to listen to in its own right.

The music follows some semblance of chronology. It does not conform to an exact date sequence but the pieces are grouped together in periods and styles of music so that one really can also get a feel for the gradual development of music as time went by.

There follows a brief introduction to each of the pieces found on the tape and some immediate guidance as to which other composers and their works you should explore if you like what you have heard. Consult the 'Top Fifty Composers' chapter for further suggestions of music: the 'Recommended Listening' list includes a selection of each composer's finest works followed by the

'Further Listening' list suggesting other works by the same composer that are perhaps not quite so well known, but are equally well worth investigating.

So, between the music on this recording and the listening-lists within the book, you should be able to get to grips with all of the more popular styles of classical music. Most people 'know what they like when they hear it' and I hope that this book, along with *Get Into Classical Music Volume 1*, will go some way towards helping you know more about classical music, without having to delve into the more formal text-books that most of us find heavy-going and unapproachable.

Another thing to bear in mind when you go into a record shop is the rather bewildering choice of so many different versions of the same piece. How do you know which one to buy?

First, there will be the choice of which orchestra or performer you most prefer and that is going to be a personal choice on your part because nearly all the top orchestras have recorded all the most popular music for many different major record companies. Orchestras from different countries do vary in their style of performance and only by hearing a few will you be able to make your choice. As a rule of thumb, however, by choosing an orchestra of the same nationality as the composer you won't go far wrong. To give you a couple of examples, I must say that I am keen on Czech music played by the Czech Philharmonic Orchestra; similarly, if you are a fan of the music of the Strauss family, you would not be disappointed by a recording by the Vienna Philharmonic Orchestra. Having said that, most of the top international orchestras can sound marvellous in works by composers of all nationalities. At the end of the day, the choice has to be yours.

Having made some kind of choice of performers, there are two other factors to bear in mind: the coupling (what else is on the record with the piece or pieces that you are after) and the value-for-money aspect. Many companies are now issuing CDs at very competitive prices, which is good to know when records and cassettes can be so horrendously overpriced. Do check how long the CD or record is. Most recording companies are trying to keep their timings between fifty-five and seventy minutes. Beware of the forty-minute albums; these are very bad value and a little bit of effort in exploring the other options available to you will ensure a much more satisfactory purchase.

Vivaldi: *Third Movement, 'Autumn', from The Four Seasons Op. 8 No. 3*

Even before Nigel Kennedy made his famous recording of *The Four Seasons*, there were literally dozens of recordings in the catalogue and this is probably one of the most popular works of all time by any composer.

Vivaldi knew that what he had written was something rather special and inscribed in the score: 'Il Cimento dell'Armonia e dell'Inventione' ('The test of harmony and invention') – the test being of his ability to portray the seasons using the medium of music. He did this with some considerable degree of success and these four mini-concertos were published in 1725 by Le Cene in Amsterdam.

Music that aimed to depict pictures, poems, stories or the elements was not really fashionable until more than a hundred years later; so this is one of the earliest and most classic examples of what is called programme music – the title given to music of this type by Liszt, who was another fine exponent. Vivaldi wrote in the margins of the players' parts helpful hints that clarify what is being depicted within each passage. For example, in '*Spring*' he has written 'the song of the birds', 'the brooks flow', 'thunderclaps' and even 'the barking dog' at exactly the point when the performer should be thinking of these things.

Vivaldi wrote hundreds of concertos for many different instruments. Those for violin, cello, guitar, organ and oboe are the most popular and, if you like what you've heard on the tape, are also well worth listening to. Other Baroque music that you may well enjoy are the works by Bach, Handel, Telemann, Scarlatti and Albinoni. Particularly recommended are Bach's *Double Violin Concerto in D minor* and the *Brandenburg Concerto No. 3*. However, if what you've really enjoyed is the sound of the solo violin, then you might also wish to start exploring the Concertos for Violin by Bach, Mendelssohn, Bruch and Tchaikovsky and then move on to those by Beethoven, Brahms, Sibelius and Berg.

Bach: *Air from Suite No. 3 in D, BWV 1068*

Familiar to anyone who has watched television in the last ten years, Bach's *Air on the G String*, as it has become known, has been used as the soundtrack to the Hamlet cigar commercials. It is the best example of relaxed music from the Baroque period that I know and was given its present title by a nineteenth-century musician who arranged it for violin and piano, confining the tune to the lowest and richest-sounding string on the fiddle – the G string.

No-one knows exactly when Bach wrote this piece, but evidence suggests that 1730–1 is about right. The beautiful soothing quality to this music can unfortunately be shattered when heard in the context of the whole piece, because many of the other movements within the suite are fast energetic dance-pieces.

If I'm in the mood for relaxing, I really do only want to hear relaxing music; and so, if you are like me, perhaps it would be worth making yourself a tape of just the slower movements from works of this period. I can thoroughly recommend the slow movements of all Bach's *Orchestral Suites*, the *Brandenburg Concertos*, and any of the Vivaldi concertos, together with Handel's *Largo* taken from the opera *Serse* and the famous *Adagio* by Albinoni. The *sarabandes* from the suites also have this relaxed, usually melancholic quality to them and definitely worth exploring would be the *Solo Cello Suites* by Bach.

Handel: *'The Arrival of the Queen of Sheba'*

With the '*Hallelujah Chorus*' from the *Messiah*, *'The Arrival of the Queen of Sheba'* is one of Handel's most famous and best-loved pieces. It is taken from his oratorio *Solomon* and was first performed at the Theatre Royal, Covent Garden, in London on 17 March 1749. Handel's oratorios are grand-scale works, this one being three acts long. Handel was a prolific composer and he completed *Solomon* in just forty days from beginning to end. The text is taken from the Book of Kings, the Second Book of Chronicles in the Old Testament and from some writings of Flavius Josephus, a first-century historian and statesman.

'*The Arrival of the Queen of Sheba*' is scored for two oboes and strings and comes at the start of Act 3. It's a brilliant musical portrayal of a grand entrance being made by the Queen, creating exactly the right atmosphere and is often used at state occasions today. If you get the chance to see this performed live, make a point of watching the oboists, who will be turning a pleasant shade of puce owing to the sustained effort that is required to play this piece!

This is a great example of instrumental music from the Baroque period and the obvious follow-ons from here include Handel's *Water Music* and his *Music for the Royal Fireworks*, together with Bach's *Brandenburg Concertos*, of which there are six.

Mozart: *Fourth Movement, Rondo, from Eine Kleine Nachtmusik, K.525*

Another very famous piece, Mozart's *Eine Kleine Nachtmusik* (*A Little Night Music*) is a suite of four movements for string orchestra. It was originally in five movements, but one has mysteriously been lost. It was also originally written to be played by only five players – string quartet and double bass – and what we hear today is not quite what Mozart had in mind when writing the piece. However, I'm sure that he would have approved since one of his main purposes was to write music that everyone could appreciate and enjoy. This piece certainly fits the bill.

Most people will also recognize the first movement of this suite. If you buy a recording of the whole piece you will not be disappointed. Mozart stopped work on his opera *Don Giovanni* especially to write this work and it has a wonderfully sunny, inspired quality to it.

Other works by Mozart that also have the same sort of character include the overture to *The Marriage of Figaro,* the *Serenade No. 7* (*'Haffner'*) and any of the *Divertimentos for Strings* (especially *K.136, K.138* and *K.239*). *Eine Kleine Nachtmusik* is an excellent introduction to the music of Mozart and if you've found this particular extract enjoyable I can confidently recommend that you explore absolutely all of Mozart's music. The obvious composer to move on to his Haydn and the same rule applies. If you like one or two of his pieces, then you are pretty well guaranteed to enjoy the lot. Try Haydn's *Trumpet Concerto* and the *Symphony No. 101*.

Beethoven: *Adagio from the 'Moonlight' Sonata Op. 27 No. 2*

As with Bach's *Air on the G String*, Beethoven played no part in giving this piano sonata its title. The famous critic Rellstab is responsible, as he once wrote that whenever he heard this work he imagined a boat bathed in moonlight on Lake Lucerne in Switzerland. Beethoven wrote the piece in 1801 for a pupil of his called Giulietta Guicciardi. It is worth noting here that Beethoven was very fond of the young girl and this could explain why he 'broke all the rules' and started the piece with a sublimely romantic slow movement. Normally one would start with a formal allegro (quick and lively) movement that would lead into a slow movement later on.

The romantic scene is set beautifully by this first movement and passion is also the mood of the last movement – which all explains why this sonata has become one of the most popular pieces in the entire piano repertoire.

Beethoven wrote thirty-two piano sonatas. They are, by and large, all wonderful works but the earlier ones are more approachable than those from No. 24 ('*Hammerklavier*') onwards. I would particularly recommend Nos. 8, 17 and 23 ('*Pathétique*', '*Tempest*' and '*Appassionata*') for first listening, going on to Nos. 24 and 31 for a more challenging, intense experience. If you've enjoyed this movement on the recording, then do go on to the *Piano Concertos* by Beethoven as a natural progression. There are five and they are all excellent. If it is the piano itself that has captured your enthusiasm, then do not miss the sonatas and concertos by Mozart and move on to the works of Chopin and Liszt. You may also like to hear Glenn Gould's recordings of the keyboard works of Bach. These are among my favourite recordings, perhaps the most outstanding being the *Goldberg Variations*.

Mendelssohn: *Scherzo from A Midsummer Night's Dream*

The overture to the suite *A Midsummer Night's Dream* was written when Mendelssohn was just seventeen years of age. He dedicated it to the Prince of Russia, the work having been commissioned by the King as the incidental music to Shakespeare's play. The remainder of the *Suite Op. 61*, from which the scherzo is taken, was written some sixteen years later, but the music has not lost any of the brilliance and youthful vitality of the earlier work.

This scherzo is typical of Mendelssohn's wonderful ability to create a magical atmosphere within the music.

If you've enjoyed this track, do explore the rest of the suite. One movement will be very familiar to you: the *Wedding March* that is played at more marriages than any other piece of music.

Other works by Mendelssohn to go on to include the *Violin Concerto*, the *Hebrides Overture* and the marvellous *Symphonies Nos. 3 and 4.* The *Violin Concerto* is one of the most popular of all violin works and contains a fantastic blend of beautiful romantic melodies with a rhythmic vitality that few composers have been able to equal. Max Bruch's *Violin Concerto* is often coupled with the Mendelssohn and is a great work, but I cannot easily lead you to other composers who wrote like Mendelssohn. He was rather exceptional.

Brahms: *Third Movement from Symphony No. 1 in C minor Op. 68*

The composer Hugo Wolf described the Brahms symphonies as 'nauseatingly stale, profoundly mendacious and mixed-up wool-gathering'. Brahms found this highly amusing as he was both irritated and bored by the high praise he had been getting from the establishment critics. The movement on this recording is a lovely example of one of the shorter movements from the four symphonies. If you like it, do listen to the complete symphony and move on to the other three.

There are wonderful symphonic works to progress to and immediate suggestions include: Rachmaninov's *Symphony No. 2*, Tchaikovsky's *Symphonies Nos. 4, 5 and 6*, the Berlioz *Symphonie fantastique* and Schumann's *Symphony No. 3*.

If you generally like the warm, autumnal, reflective nature of the music from the *Symphony No. 1*, I can thoroughly recommend the *Academic Festival Overture*, the *Violin Concerto* and the two *Piano Concertos* by Brahms, but I would add that this music is not as immediately accessible as that of Mozart or Haydn. After several listenings, however, it can be the source of great enjoyment. Brahms is emotionally challenging and many people find his music very moving. My advice is that it's well worth getting to know.

Tchaikovsky: *Valse from Serenade for Strings Op. 48*

Most famous for his 'love theme' from the *Fantasy Overture 'Romeo and Juliet'*, Tchaikovsky wrote the *Serenade for Strings* in 1880. The piece was warmly received by critics and audience alike and it is a charming, essentially happy work that avoids the use of minor (sad-sounding) keys all the way through. It's quite often performed (and recorded) alongside the work of the same name by Antonin Dvořák, who is most famous for the slow movement from his *'New World' Symphony,* perhaps best-known as the theme from the Hovis commercials on television.

Tchaikovsky was a truly cosmopolitan composer and within the *Serenade* he reflects his love for three of his favourite countries. The first movement is entitled *Pezzo in forma di sonatina* and is obviously Italianate in flavour; while the *Valse*, heard on this recording, has distinctly French overtones. The fourth and last movement interestingly incorporates a pair of Russian themes from his native land.

Tchaikovsky is also well known for his symphonic and ballet music and these are well worth listening to. Try the incidental music to *Swan Lake, Sleeping Beauty* and the *Nutcracker Suite* and then move on to the *Symphonies Nos. 4, 5 and 6*. Of course, you should not overlook the *1812 Overture* or the wonderful *Romeo and Juliet*. If this sort of music is your kind of thing then try Rachmaninov's *Piano Concertos* and *Symphonies*. However, if what you've really enjoyed is the lovely sweet and rich sound of the string orchestra, there is plenty more music by other composers in a similar vein. The best examples are to be found in the *Serenades* by Dvořák and Elgar, together with the *Fantasia on a Theme by Thomas Tallis* by Vaughan Williams. Elgar's exquisite *Introduction and Allegro* is also among my favourites and is commonly coupled with his *Chanson du matin* and *Chanson de nuit*. One other piece not to be missed under any circumstances is the *Adagio* by Samuel Barber, which is one of the most haunting pieces played by a string orchestra that you are ever likely to come across.

Rachmaninov: *First Movement from Piano Concerto No. 2 in C minor*

Rachmaninov was an extraordinary man who naturally follows on from Chopin and Liszt as another of the truly great writers (and performers) of music for the piano. Chopin was always poetic, Liszt was a showman and technical wizard, while Rachmaninov was impassive and morose and barely wished to acknowledge his public. Rachmaninov is probably my favourite composer. The piece found here on this recording is typical of his style – highly charged, richly harmonic and with a yearning quality that gives it an emotional intensity with which everyone can identify.

The *Piano Concertos* (particularly the second and third) are among many people's favourite works and they really should not be missed. The *Piano Concerto No. 2* came to the public's attention as the soundtrack to the film *Brief Encounter*, while the *Symphony No. 2* is a work in a very similar vein.

Other works that you could go on to, having heard the music of Rachmaninov, will depend on whether it's the lyrical romantic style or the dramatic, more impetuous Russian-sounding quality to the music which appeals to you. For lovers of the romantic-lyrical aspect, go on to Tchaikovsky's *Piano Concerto No. 1*, *Romeo and Juliet* and the *Symphonies Nos. 4, 5 and 6*, and also any of the piano music by Brahms. If, however, you are more interested in the Russian, dramatic element, then your next step might be to listen to the music of Prokofiev. His *Piano Concerto No. 3* and the ballet music to *Romeo and Juliet* are among my own favourites, as well as the suite *Lieutenant Kije*, an extract from which is also to be found on this recording.

Chopin: *Fantasie Impromptu Op. 66 in C sharp minor*

Chopin, the great poetic master of the piano, wrote an enormous amount of music for solo piano in addition to his two concertos for piano with orchestra and a selection of works for various combinations of instruments. The *Fantasie Impromptu* is one of the most famous examples of his work and contains all the great elements of his style: Poetry, virtuosity and romanticism all in one short piece. The work was not published during Chopin's lifetime because he considered it might too closely have resembled a piece by a now relatively unknown composer, Moscheles. The piece was written in 1834 when Chopin was only twenty-four years old and coincidentally the theme is not dissimilar to that of the last movement of Beethoven's *'Moonlight' Sonata.*

Among my other favourite Chopin pieces are the *Ballade No. 1 in G minor*, the *Berceuse* and all of the *Nocturnes*. Perhaps I should add that I find it very difficult to list any of his music that I'm not keen on and can pretty well recommend the whole catalogue! Liszt is often paired with Chopin and these two were the leading protagonists in the Romantic Movement where the piano was concerned. Liszt's *Transcendental Études* are beautiful, as are the *Consolations*. Other composers to move on to, if you like the sound of the romantic piano, are Brahms, Schumann and Rachmaninov. Try the *Ballades Op. 10* by Brahms, the *Fantasia in C Op. 17* by Schumann or any of Rachmaninov's *Preludes Op. 32*.

Dvořák: Slavonic Dance, Op. 46 No. 1

Dvořák (pronounced 'Vorjacques') had to struggle to make a name for himself, but eventually was given his first major break by the celebrated composer Johannes Brahms. Brahms heard a set of vocal duets that Dvořák had written and was so impressed that he persuaded his own publisher, Simrock, to sign him up and put the works into print. Simrock were delighted with the recommendation and immediately commissioned Dvořák to write a collection of *Slavonic Dances* for piano duet that were to be modelled on the *Hungarian Dances* by Brahms. This he did together with a whole host of similar works for orchestra and various combinations of instruments, all of which were a tremendous success. The *Dance No. 1* on this recording is the perfect example of Dvořák's unique talent for writing spirited Czech tunes with wonderful rhythmic vitality and also demonstrates his gift for creating colourful orchestrations from the piano works.

Going on from here, his symphonies and the *Cello Concerto* possess similar inherent qualities, but in a slightly less obvious way. The *Symphonies Nos. 7 and 9* are my own favourites and you would also be well advised to listen to the works of his contemporary Smetana while Janáček's *Sinfonietta* and the *Moravian Dances* are also quite remarkable works.

Nationalistic music is inspiring and colourful and there are excellent examples from the Russian School in particular. Mussorgsky's *Pictures at an Exhibition* and Prokofiev's *Romeo and Juliet* should not be missed. Then, the Hungarian Zoltán Kodály wrote the *Hary Janos Suite* and the *Dances of Galanta*, which are popular favourites with audiences throughout the world. From Scandinavia, Grieg's *Peer Gynt* and *Holberg Suites* are classics, as well as his *Piano Concerto;* while the twentieth-century composer Carl Nielsen also wrote some excellent music, including the concertos for flute and clarinet. Do listen to the music of the Finnish composer Jean Sibelius. The *Symphonies Nos. 1, 5 and 7* immediately spring to mind, while his most famous work, *Finlandia*, is a piece that perfectly captures the spirit of his native land.

Prokofiev: *Troika from Lieutenant Kije*

Lieutenant Kije is the fictional hero of a film made in 1933, for which Prokofiev was commissioned to write the score. The story-line is perfectly matched by Prokofiev's ironic, witty style of writing. The plot of the film revolves around an error made by a government clerk who wrongly enters the name Lieutenant Kije on the official army list. In order to avoid having to admit to such an error and the undoubted furore this would cause, a tale of deception and invention there unfolds, only ending with the apparent 'death' of the lieutenant. The *Troika* from the suite depicts the sleigh ride while Lieutenant Kije is on his honeymoon and Prokofiev's brilliant music, so colourfully orchestrated with sleigh bells, has made this a firm favourite around Christmas-time. It serves as a lovely introduction to the music of this most celebrated of Russian composers.

His score for the ballet *Romeo and Juliet* is a classic. Also well worth hearing is the *Piano Concerto No. 3*. This is Russian music at its best and, if you find this style appealing, other works to be explored include Mussorgsky's *Pictures at an Exhibition* and the *Night on a Bare Mountain*, Stravinsky's *Firebird Suite* and his ballet music to *Pulcinella*. Rimsky Korsakov is another composer who had an enormous flair for writing nationalistic music: Russian, Spanish, Arabian – you name it! Of particular interest are his *Coq d'or, Scheherazade* and *Capriccio Espagnol*. Moving on to the slightly more esoteric but no less enjoyable, one should also listen to Borodin's *Polovtsian Dances* from *Prince Igor*, while Glazunov's *The Seasons* and Respighi's *Fountains of Rome* are also well worth taking in.

Debussy: *Clair de lune*

The 'Father of the French Impressionists School', Debussy was one of the most important innovators in writing for orchestra and piano. Whereas Chopin and Liszt had taken the technical possibilities of the piano to their limit, Debussy managed to find his own niche by exploring and developing the possibilities of tonal nuance that lay within the instrument's capabilities. He applied a similar approach to his technique of orchestration and created ways of making the sound of both the piano and the orchestra quite radically different from those who had preceded him.

This has served to be a major source of inspiration for all composers who have followed him and he has been extremely influential. *Clair de lune* was originally written for piano and I have chosen this particular piece to demonstrate how well the music also sounds when played by an orchestra. His most famous orchestral works include *La Mer, Nocturnes* and *Prélude à l'après-midi d'un faune.* These are all wonderful, atmospheric and sensuously beautiful pieces that provide an excellent introduction to French music and music from the Impressionists in particular.

Debussy wrote a lot of piano music, including two volumes of *Preludes*, a suite entitled *Pour le piano* and a number of other shorter pieces of which the *Deux Arabesques* are among my own favourites. Ravel, the other major composer from within this group, was a master of writing for the piano who also possessed the gift of creating beautiful new sounds and colours using the orchestra. Among his finest piano works are *Gaspard de la nuit, Miroirs, Pavane pour une infante défunte* and *Alborado del gracioso.*

However, it is in the field of orchestration that Debussy and Ravel were so highly innovative, using the orchestra as an instrument in its own right. They actually did create new sounds and have been a most important influence on all composers since. Debussy's *La Mer* and the *Prélude à l'après-midi d'un faune* are essential listening, as are Ravel's celebrated *Bolero*, the *Daphnis and Chloé* ballet suites, *La Valse* and the *Rapsodie espagnole.*

Elgar: *'Nimrod' from the 'Enigma' Variations Op. 36*

Written in 1899, the *'Enigma' Variations* was Elgar's first full-scale work for orchestra and for an essentially self-taught composer it was an incredible achievement. It demonstrates his talent as a master of orchestration and the work is used as a showpiece by many leading symphony orchestras all around the world.

There is a curious story attached to the *'Enigma' Variations.* The main tune on which the variations are based incorporates a very famous melody, the identity of which Elgar would never reveal even to his closest friends. The work is also unusually autobiographical in that each of the fourteen variations portrays the character of one of his friends (one of whom is a dog!). Nimrod, the hunter, is an Elgarian pun on A. J. Jaeger (German for 'hunter'), who was one of Elgar's closest friends and also his publisher. This is a beautifully romantic and emotional piece and if you enjoy it you will find similar pleasure in the *Cello and Violin Concertos*, together with Elgar's works for string orchestra like the *Introduction and Allegro* and the *Serenade.* Other composers to go on to include Vaughan Williams – try the *Fantasia on a Theme by Thomas Tallis* – and Delius in his '*The Walk to the Paradise Garden*'. Gerald Finzi's *Clarinet Concerto* is another beautiful work embodying similar characteristics; but if you are especially taken by the Edwardian nationalistic element in Elgar's music, then you must go on to his *Pomp and Circumstance Marches*, particularly No. 1: '*Land of Hope and Glory*'.

Mahler: *Fourth Movement from Symphony No. 1 in D*

The *Symphonies Nos. 1 and 4* are perhaps the most approachable of Mahler's nine complete symphonies (he started a tenth that has since been completed by Derek Cooke). Many people have also become familiar with one extract from his music, the *Adagietto* from *Symphony No. 5* which was made famous in the Visconti film *Death in Venice* starring Dirk Bogarde. There are also innumerable songs, many of which have orchestral accompaniments and Mahler was a master of writing for the voice; particularly appealing are his *Kindertotenlieder, Das Lied von der Erde* (*The Song of the Earth*) and *Das Knaben Wunderhorn.*

This, his first symphony, was completed in 1888, when he was twenty-eight years of age. It is autobiographical music (like most of his output) and is said to reflect his emotional thoughts and feelings after a broken love-affair with Johanna Richter. The work is scored for a large orchestra (a common trait in Mahler's orchestral music) and ends with a magnificent triumphal display of the theme being played by seven horns.

Other composers to whom one would immediately be led by this example might include Bruckner, who also wrote large-scale symphonies – they are long, expansive and highly developed pieces of romantic music. These are all highly recommended if you have time on your hands, but be warned: Mahler and Bruckner symphonies are *very long*.

Wagner: *Introduction to Act 3 of Lohengrin*

Wagner had a very fixed idea about what form the preludes to the acts of his operas should take. In fact he felt so strongly about the subject that he was rather pompously moved to write: 'My Preludes must consist of the "elements" and not be dramatic like [Beethoven's]

Leonora overtures – or the drama becomes superfluous!' The *Introduction to Act 3* of *Lohengrin*, featured here, is full of life and is an excellent example of Wagner's masterly use of the orchestra in his writing. The music sets the scene for the wedding festivities of Lohengrin and Elsa, the main characters in the opera. There are a number of very fine recordings available, consisting of all the preludes and overtures to Wagner's operas and these will serve as a marvellous introduction to his music in general, as well as giving you a good idea of the flavour of each opera.

Among the most popular is the overture to *Die Meistersinger von Nürnberg* and the theme from *Tristan und Isolde*, while another of my favourites is the piece for small orchestra entitled *Siegfried Idyll*, first performed on Christmas morning 1870 following the birth of Wagner's son Siegfried.

Wagner's operas are grand-scale pieces that are not always immediately accessible. My advice is to try the preludes and overtures first. One of the other major operatic composers writing at this time was Verdi and you may well find his works to be instantly more approachable; the music from *Aida* and *La Traviata* will provide a good sample of his music. Best of all, save up and go and see one of the operas live and enjoy the full impact of the spectacle. Next best is to hire a video; this is probably the most cost-effective way of getting into these composers, while not being as immediately exciting as seeing their works performed live on stage.

Puccini: *'Nessun dorma' from Turandot*

Cast your mind back to the summer of 1990 and the World Cup in Italy and you surely will not have forgotten the association made between Pavarotti's heartrending performance of Puccini's aria '*Nessun dorma*', from the opera *Turandot*, and the emotional outbursts on the football-field.

As you probably know, operas are often very long works and the extract that Pavarotti has made famous is just one song from an opera that actually takes almost three hours to perform. Do not be put off! The rest of the opera is wonderful and it's well worth the effort of going to see it live. *La Bohème* is the natural follow-on, also by Puccini and this opera, too, is full of good tunes.

Opera is a wide subject that requires a book all to itself but, if you are among the five million or so people who found '*Nessun dorma*' so moving that you just had to buy it, do listen to other Puccini operas and perhaps move on to *La Traviata* or *Aida* by Verdi and *Carmen* by Bizet. Rossini and Donizetti were also excellent tunesmiths in the lighter operatic style and almost anything of theirs is worth hearing.

Gershwin: *Rhapsody in Blue*

George Gershwin is probably the most famous composer to have successfully combined the elements of jazz with those of regular classical music. The *Rhapsody in Blue* is his most famous work and starts off with the 'classic' clarinet solo that has become a trademark for clarinet players over the years. Gershwin was himself a brilliant virtuoso pianist and the writing contained in this work is a challenge for even today's top concert pianists.

The piece was completed in 1924 when Gershwin was just twenty-four years old, having achieved world renown as the composer of the hit song '*Swanee*', performed by Al Jolson.

Move on to any of his works; they are all highly entertaining. Particularly enjoyable are *An American in Paris, Piano Concerto in F* and the opera *Porgy and Bess*. Other composers and their works that you will enjoy if you like the works of Gershwin include Leonard Bernstein's *West Side Story* and Copland's *Clarinet Concerto* (which was dedicated to the celebrated jazz clarinettist Benny Goodman).

Chapter Three

The Top Fifty Composers

Baroque Music, 1685–1750

Many people will be familiar with Vivaldi's *Four Seasons*, particularly after the extraordinary success of Nigel Kennedy's album promoting the work of 'Viv', as he has been affectionately renamed. Another very famous piece from this period that has been presented on British television screens for many years now as the soundtrack for Hamlet cigar commercials is Bach's *Air on the G String* – one of our Starter Top Ten already discussed.

This wonderful music began to happen in the late seventeenth century and in fact 1685 proved to be a very significant year: It was the year when Bach, Handel and Scarlatti were born. Vivaldi and Telemann had been born a few years earlier. The works of Vivaldi, Bach and Handel are really the first ones to explore, followed by those of Telemann and Scarlatti; but I should stress that there were scores of composers writing good music at the time and there's a huge catalogue for you to enjoy if you are keen on the music of the Baroque composers.

Antonio Vivaldi (1678–1741)

Born in Venice, Vivaldi appears to have been quite a remarkable character. He started learning the violin at a very early age, being taught by his father and immediately showed great promise, later becoming one of the most celebrated violinist-composers to have lived.

At the age of fifteen he started his training for the priesthood, which took almost ten years to complete and when finally he became a fully fledged priest in 1703, he promptly decided to give up saying mass on the rather spurious grounds of ill health. Apparently it was not uncommon for him to leave a service in mid-celebration, complaining of chest pains, only to rush off and scribble down a new tune for a concerto.

Although Vivaldi's main priorities were writing and performing music, he retained an almost life-long association with one of the major charitable institutions in Venice, which was concerned with looking after and educating young orphaned girls – of whom there were hundreds in the city at that time. This place, La Pietà, as it was known, was to become something of a mini-conservatoire of music. The children were educated with a definite bias towards music, all taking lessons on string instruments from Vivaldi and other musicians. This led to numerous concerts given by the youngsters of a remarkably high standard and these became something of a regular attraction in Venice. Vivaldi played a major role in the preparation and staging of these concerts and also brought in many other well-known composers and musicians of the day to take part.

From 1703, aged twenty-five, he concentrated on composing music. His first pieces were published a couple of years later and he embarked upon what was to turn out to be a highly successful and rewarding career. Always travelling and extremely busy, Vivaldi liked not only to compose the music but also to take an active part in rehearsing and conducting the performances.

Between 1703 and his death in 1741 he wrote an astonishing 750 works, most of which are of exceptional quality. The most famous is that for violin and orchestra, *The Four Seasons* and he is perhaps best-known for his pieces written in a similar vein: the concertos for violins, guitar, bassoon and cello. There are, in addition, forty-six operas listed in the catalogue (although Vivaldi claimed to have written nearly a hundred; the remaining fifty or so are now lost), dozens of works for miscellaneous wind instruments, trio sonatas, vocal pieces and a whole host of small chamber works.

Recommended Listening

The Four Seasons (O)
The Flute Concertos Op. 10 (O)
Gloria in D, RV 589 (V/O)
Concerto in A minor for Cello and Strings (O)
Twelve Concertos Op. 4 (O)

Further Listening

Concerto for Viola d'amore, RV 540 (O)
Trio Sonata 'La Follia' (Ch)
Sinfonia, RV 149 (O)
Five Recorder Concertos, RV 441–5 (O)
'L'Estro Armonico' Concertos Op. 3 (O)

Johann Sebastian Bach (1685–1750)

In the early part of the sixteenth century the Bach family were quite well known throughout northern Germany as a family of accomplished musicians and they achieved widespread fame when young Johann Sebastian's talents came to light. As a boy he apparently had a fantastic soprano singing voice and always took the leading roles in the church and school choirs. He started composing fairly early in his life; his first main works, including the *Preludes and Variations* for organ, were composed between the ages of seventeen and twenty. The organ was an instrument for which Bach wrote superlatively; he was a great lover of church music in general and was regarded as one of the finest organists of the day. Brought up with a strong association with the church, he was always involved in church music of one kind or another as a singer and an organist. He wrote his marvellous series of cantatas for the Sunday services at the Church of Bonifacius in Arnstadt where he was appointed organist (his first job) and these works are probably the finest of their type.

Bach was always in demand and held a succession of excellent jobs throughout his lifetime. These included celebrated posts at the courts of Duke Wilhelm Ernst of Weimar and Prince Leopold of Cöthen. His last employment was as the Cantor of the Thomasschule in Leipzig. Life, however, was not always a bed of roses.

In the early years Bach was heavily influenced by the composer Buxtehude (another great writer for the organ) and he left his job in Arnstadt to go and have lessons with the maestro. This turned into a four-month sabbatical, and Bach was in deep trouble with his employers when he returned, for not only had his presence been missed but he'd come back writing in quite an advanced and unusual style that was not exactly what was required. It was actually great music that was a little ahead of its time.

So Bach moved on to a job in Weimar, which afforded him greater artistic freedom. His main duties were as court organist and chamber musician to the reigning Duke Wilhelm Ernst and he subsequently got the job of *Konzertmeister* (conductor) to the court orchestra in his last three years of service. It was at the beginning of this period of work that he wrote some of his most famous organ pieces, including the marvellous *Passacaglia and Fugue in C minor*. The top job at these various courts was invariably as *Kapellmeister* and this position became vacant in 1716 at Weimar. Much to Bach's annoyance, he was not offered the job and he immediately started to look for another position, ending up at the court of Prince Leopold of Cöthen. This move was the subject of some controversy, as Bach's Weimar employers were upset by his reasons for wanting to leave and they refused to let him go – at one point even having him arrested. Finally good sense prevailed and Bach moved on to Cöthen where he spent many happy years.

This period of work at Cöthen was when Bach wrote probably his finest music: *The Brandenburg Concertos* (so called because they were dedicated to Duke Christian Ludwig of Brandenburg), the violin concertos, the suites for orchestra and much of the chamber music. Bach got on very well with Prince Leopold and it was some five years before he had the urge to move on again. This followed a great tragedy in his life, when his wife died while he was away on tour. Bach returned to find her dead and buried.

He married again, a young girl called Anna Magdalena, and in 1722 applied for a job at the Thomasschule in Leipzig. The competition for this job was fierce, with Bach's rivals being two other celebrated musicians of the day: Telemann and Graupner. The council making the appointment chose Telemann but, following his withdrawal and the fact that Graupner could not actually take up the job, they eventually settled for Bach. His responsibilities were many: Teaching, composing, conducting and supervising the musical activities of a couple of churches. During this time Bach's son Carl Philipp Emanuel – Bach had some twenty children during his life – was gaining great respect and went to work for the Prussian Emperor Frederick the Great. This, in turn, helped Bach senior's career and when he visited Frederick's court he was a big success, both socially and professionally.

The year before his death in 1750, Bach went temporarily blind. He regained his sight only ten days before his death, which was caused by a stroke. Like many a famous composer, he was buried in an unmarked grave that was only rediscovered when the churchyard of Johanneskirche, Leipzig, was being extended. Today Bach is revered by music-lovers all over the world as one of the finest composers ever to have lived, writing what has been described as 'pure' music. His works, both sacred and secular, have a totally unique quality and spirit about them and listed below is a selection of some of the real 'greats'. In addition to what is listed there are some 295 cantatas, innumerable organ works and hundreds of smaller works for various combinations of instruments. His skill at writing for keyboard instruments and for choirs also had a significant effect on all composers who followed him – even to the present day. He was indeed a true innovator and genius.

Recommended Listening

Brandenburg Concerto No. 3 BWV 1048 (O)
Double Violin Concerto, BWV 1043 (O)
Mass in B minor, BWV 232 (V/O)
Toccata and Fugue in D minor, BWV 565 (Org)
Solo Suites for Cello, BWV 1007–12 (I)

Further Listening

St Matthew Passion, BWV 244 (V/O)
Passacaglia and Fugue in C minor, BWV 582 (Org)
Goldberg Variations, BWV 988 (I)
Italian Concerto in F, BWV 971 (I)
Suite No. 2 in B minor, BWV 1067 (O)

George Frideric Handel (1685–1759)

Handel is often regarded as being a British composer. Although born in Halle, Germany, he spent much of his life in London and lived in a beautiful house in Brook Street where he composed many of his finest works. In 1727 he applied for British citizenship, which was immediately granted and Handel assumed the role of composer of music for royal occasions. This led to him writing four fantastic anthems for the coronation of George II, perhaps the most famous of which is '*Zadok the Priest*', which has been performed at nearly every British coronation since. His music is wonderfully melodic and holds a unique place in the repertoire of the Baroque composers.

Handel was the son of a rather boorish 'barber-surgeon' who was distinctly uneasy about his son having anything to do with the music business. It was intended by Handel senior that his son should become a lawyer and young George Frideric was discouraged from pursuing any serious interest in music.

He was already a very capable organist by the age of ten and after some pressure from his employer, Handel senior finally agreed to allow his son to have some music lessons from an eminent organist and teacher in Halle. The boy quickly became proficient on the oboe and the violin, as well as on the organ and harpsichord and also took lessons in composition. It soon became quite clear that he was highly gifted. It was at about this time that his father died, but his influence endured and Handel enrolled to study law at the University of Halle in 1702. He was obviously not interested in law and started to apply himself seriously to his music. He became the organist of the cathedral but later moved on to Hamburg where he worked at the opera house in the Goosemarket.

While he was there he struck up a friendship with a young man called Johann Matheson. The two became close friends and on one occasion, hearing that the celebrated organist Buxtehude was about to retire from his job in Lübeck, they set off on a journey with the intention of one or the other of them securing the post. It turned out that the person who was to get the job would have to marry Buxtehude's daughter, who was not exactly a prime catch. Handel and his friend Matheson both had a change of heart and made their way immediately back to Hamburg!

Handel and Matheson's friendship then suffered a serious setback. They fell out over who was to direct an opera and the situation had to be resolved by fighting a duel in full view of the public in the Goosemarket. Neither composer was seriously hurt and they soon made up their differences but Matheson is quoted as reporting that, had he not had the good fortune to stab Handel directly on a broad metal coat-button, the consequences could have been fatal.

It's interesting to note that even in Handel's day the idea of musical competitions was very much in evidence. Today we have the BBC Young Musician of the Year, the Tchaikovsky Prize and major competitions in Munich, Leeds, New York and so on. In Handel's day there was a similar interest in such contests and in Rome the Count Ottoboni staged one such competition to ascertain whether Handel or Domenico Scarlatti was the finer performer. The results of this bizarre event are not totally clear, although it seems the general consensus of opinion was that, although Handel was second to none on the organ, both were equally gifted on the harpsichord.

Handel was very prolific and was particularly interested in writing operas and oratorios. So interested that he set up his own opera company called the Royal Academy of Music. This was based at the King's Theatre in the Haymarket in London and in the early days was an enormous success. The company was established to present operas in Italian, but in 1728 John Gay staged his *Beggar's Opera* at John Rich's theatre in Lincoln's Inn Fields. This opera, sung in English, was very well received and appealed to a much wider audience than the previously popular Italian operas. Presenting operas based on folk culture, in English, became so popular that support for Handel's Royal Academy of Music tailed off and within six months he became bankrupt.

Handel was undeterred and set about re-forming his company, engaging new singers from Italy and staging various new works together with a selection of past successes. Things did not go too well until he put on his own piece, *Alexander's Feast*, in 1735. However, he seems to have learnt his lesson from these experiences and like any good businessman turned his hand to providing what the public wanted. This led to more oratorios in English, of which *Messiah* is his most famous, from which most people are at least familiar with the '*Hallelujah Chorus*'. Handel went over to Dublin in 1741 to stage *Messiah* and it brought the house down – a reaction that was repeated wherever it was performed. A few years later he wrote another of his best-known works, the *Music for the Royal Fireworks*. These triumphs generated so much money for Handel that he was easily able to pay off the debts that had accrued from his Italian opera failures at the Royal Academy and he lived his last years in a considerable degree of comfort.

The now familiar feature of famous musicians 'doing their bit' for the world around them was also very much in evidence in Handel's day and he himself donated the proceeds of an annual performance of *Messiah* to the Foundling Hospital as well as providing an organ for their chapel. Handel's health began to fail at this time but, though he eventually became totally blind, he still gave concerts as an organ soloist and even as a conductor of his own works. The last performance he was to take part in was of *Messiah* at Covent Garden, but he was taken ill at the end of the evening and died at home in Brook Street a week later, on 14 April 1759.

It was always Handel's wish that he should have a private funeral, but this was for some reason ignored and over three thousand people were present at an elaborate state funeral service at Westminster Abbey.

Recommended Listening

Music for the Royal Fireworks (O)
The Water Music (O)
Messiah (Or)
'*Zadok the Priest*' (V/O)
Acis and Galatea (Op)

Further Listening

Concerti Grossi Op. 6 Nos. 1–12 (O)
Organ Concertos Op.4 (O)
'*The Arrival of the Queen of Sheba*' (O)
The Halle Flute Sonatas Nos. 1–3 (I)
Ode for St Cecilia's Day (V/O)

Where to Go from Here in the Baroque Style

It is worth delving into the music of any of the following composers. They all wrote fine music and there are literally hundreds of records to choose from in the shops. In order to make your task a little easier when faced with a row of CDs, I would particularly recommend albums containing collections of works by the following so that you can get a feel for which composers you enjoy the most and then make more selective purchases after that.

Recommended Composers

Telemann
D. Scarlatti
A. Scarlatti
Corelli
Couperin
Pergolesi
Sammartini
Boismortier
Manfredini
Rameau
Lully

The Classical Period, 1750–1827

Music from the Classical Period incorporates the works of the great masters, Mozart, Haydn, Schubert and Beethoven, which have formed the standard repertoire of classical musicians around the world for the last hundred and fifty years.

Wolfgang Amadeus Mozart (1756–91)

The film *Amadeus* did a great job in bringing the music of probably the most celebrated composer of all time to the attention of millions of people the world over. The story of Mozart's life made great viewing and, even if it was a little over the top in places, the film depicted the character and antics of this unquestioned genius in a very down-to-earth way. For those who are keen to know the historical accuracy of the film, it's probably true to say that the strong emphasis given to the feud between Mozart and the composer Salieri was rather exaggerated. While there was a definite sense of rivalry between the two of them, the film did overplay this angle for dramatic effect. The music soundtrack, exquisitely played by the Academy of St Martin-in-the-Fields conducted by Sir Neville Marriner, is one of the best introductions to Mozart's work that I can think of. There are extracts from several of the symphonies, the *Requiem*, the piano concertos and some memorable bits from the operas. If you haven't seen *Amadeus*, make the effort to rent the video. You won't be disappointed.

Apart from the fact that he was a true genius, Mozart was a completely normal chap in every other way. In addition to writing music, his main preoccupations in life were wine, women and song! He liked nothing better than to be out socializing, having a few beers with his friends and he positively delighted in writing and performing the popular music of the day. I cannot overstress this point:

Mozart was the eighteenth-century equivalent of the pop stars of today. He wrote music for the people and it is only the social stigmas that have been built up over the last few hundred years that have placed such music in the hands of the upper middle classes and alienated it from everyday folk. Good examples of his down-to-earth approach to life are to be found in the drinking songs that he wrote while out with his friends. These were recently unearthed by scholars at Harvard University and have to some extent been 'hushed up' in an attempt to avoid shattering people's illusions about this most hallowed of composers. The first in a set of three songs, apparently written while actually in a bar, graphically depicts Mozart's vulgar sense of humour. The title is 'Lick My Backside, Quickly, Quickly' and it is followed in the same set by other songs with lines too obscene to mention. So forget the vision of this handsome, beautifully dressed court musician, earnestly at work over the score of an opera or mass and remember that here we have an ordinary man of exceptional talent who, underneath it all, was at his most comfortable socially with his drinking partners, singing their equivalent of today's rugby songs.

Mozart was born into a very musical family in Salzburg on 27 January 1756, the son of a highly talented violinist-composer, Leopold, who was in the service of the Prince Archbishop of Salzburg. Being a professional musician himself, Leopold quickly spotted the precocious talent of the young Mozart and many of the standard text-books on classical music contain romantic stories of the three-year-old Mozart practising the piano and starting to compose his first pieces. Those of you who have had three year old children may find this a little hard to believe but it is a good story, even if it's not true. Leopold Mozart firmly believed that his son's talent was a divine gift and this, coupled with the fact that there should have been money to be made out of having such an extraordinary child prodigy, led him to arrange a tour of all the European courts in order to show off his extraordinary ability.

From the age of six, the young Mozart was travelling around Europe giving concerts in palaces and courts of the aristocracy as well as a series of public concerts, all of which were very well received. For some reason all this fame and adulation never made Mozart anything like a rich man. He was constantly in financial trouble, having to beg for money from friends and write music very much 'to order' just to make a living.

Mozart married – against the wishes of his father – a girl called Constanze. They had a baby nine months later which did not survive for very long. A troublesome period in Mozart's life then followed wherein he began to be desperately short of money. It was at about this time, when he was living in Vienna, that he joined the Freemasons, an association that was later to be something of a lifeline for him.

Although he'd fallen out with his father at the time of his marriage, the young Mozart was deeply affected by his death. This was in the year that Wolfgang had composed one of his most successful operas, *The Marriage of Figaro*; but, even though things were, on the face of it, going very well musically, Mozart still was not making very much money and any money he did make didn't last long. He was depressed at having to make ends meet by teaching and even that was proving to be more and more difficult, so he had to start borrowing money from friends and from the wealthier Masons at his lodge. This situation continued right up until Mozart's death at the tragically young age of thirty five. Things got worse in the last few years of his life, when his wife became very ill and doctors' fees were added to his financial and emotional burdens. One of the last pieces that Mozart was to write was, coincidentally, his *Requiem* and sadly this was never completed.

His funeral was definitely not that of a celebrated composer. He was buried in an unmarked grave; none of the mourners from the service went from the cathedral to the churchyard where he was buried and the location of his grave is still to this day unknown.

Thankfully, his music lives on and we are left with an extraordinarily large catalogue of works that display his unique gift for writing music that really is an incredible mixture of joy and beauty, often tinged with poignancy and sorrow. This vast catalogue of music was put in order by a man called Köchel; hence each of the works has what is called a Köchel number or a 'K' number attached to it. I have included them in the list of recommended listening for your future guidance.

Mozart wrote so much brilliant music that it is difficult to know where to start in recommending specific pieces to listen to. I include here my favourite examples of his finest symphonic music, the piano concertos, solo instrumental, chamber, vocal and operatic music and these will give a good start to anyone wanting to explore this vast catalogue of truly great music. If you like the piece of Mozart on the CD/tape, you will almost certainly enjoy any of his music – you really can't go wrong.

Recommended Listening

Symphonies Nos. 39, 40 and 41 (K. 543, K. 550, K. 551) (O)
Piano Concerto No. 21 in C major, K. 467 (O)
Clarinet Quintet, K. 485 (Ch)
The Marriage of Figaro, K. 492 (Op)
Eine Kleine Nachtmusik, K. 525 (O)

Further Listening

'Gran Partita', K. 361 (Ch)
Oboe Quartet, K. 370 (Ch)
Piano Concerto No. 20 in D minor, K. 466 (O)
Dissonance String Quartet, K. 465 (Ch)
Requiem, K. 626 (V/O)

Franz Josef Haydn (1732–1809)

Unlike Mozart, Haydn did not come from a musical background at all. He was taught to read music by a cousin and joined the choir of St Stephen's Cathedral in Vienna, from which he was dismissed at the age of sixteen! He had a difficult start in life and, at the beginning of his career, certainly fitted the image of the hard-at-work composer struggling to make ends meet, starving in a garret.

He managed to obtain one or two lessons in singing and composition from Nicola Porpora, a relatively famous Italian composer, developed his technique and started writing small-scale works in the form of chamber music, mainly string quartets. Haydn established a good reputation fairly quickly and landed a job as the director of music to Count Morizin. The money was poor, but at least it was a secure start for the young composer. Sadly, shortly after getting married, Haydn was made redundant, but fate was to play a hand in his being offered a job at the court of Prince Esterhazy, where he stayed until 1790 and wrote much of his finest music. He eventually ended up with the prestigious job of *Kapellmeister* to the Esterhazys, who looked after Haydn very well. The musicians there were thought to be about the best in the country at the time and consequently this inspired him to write consistently great music for the orchestra, for the choir and for small groups of instrumentalists playing chamber music and providing *harmoniemusik* (background music) for state functions and banquets.

Haydn was very loyal to his employer, possibly to the detriment of his career in that he turned down many opportunities to travel the world. However, after his period of employment with the Esterhazys ended, he went to London at the invitation of the famous violinist-impresario Salomon and this was a great success. Haydn became friendly with the royal family, his lifestyle was lavish and he had a most comfortable existence – unlike Mozart! This disparity is most clearly reflected when comparing the music of the two composers. Haydn's is generally less emotionally charged and often has a more 'happy' quality to it, whereas with Mozart there's often an inner sadness and poignancy showing through. Haydn was writing at the time when Mozart was at his best and the two held each other in high regard, occasionally even performing together. In fact there is a famous story of a conversation that Haydn had with Mozart's father during which Haydn acclaimed Mozart as being the 'greatest composer I know, personally or by reputation'.

Haydn's music played a significant role in the long-term development of classical music, particularly in the fields of the symphony, the oratorio and the string quartet. He wrote an astonishing 104 symphonies, 80 string quartets and numerous oratorios including the celebrated *Creation* and *The Seasons*. In addition there are piano, violin, cello and wind instrument concertos, instrumental works, piano sonatas, masses and a whole host of small-scale pieces for odd combinations of instruments.

Recommended Listening

Symphonies Nos. 94 ('Surprise') and 100 ('Military') (O)
String Quartet Op. 55/2 No. 67 ('Lark') (Ch)
Trumpet Concerto in E flat (O)
Piano Sonatas Nos. 58, 60, 61 (I)
The Creation (Or)

Further Listening

Symphonies Nos. 6, 7 and 8
('Le Midi', 'Le Matin' and 'Le Soir') (O)
String Quartets Nos. 77 and 78 ('Emperor' and 'Sunrise') (Ch)
The Cello Concertos in C and D major (O)
Piano Sonata No. 47 in B minor (I)
The Seasons (Or)

Ludwig van Beethoven (1770–1827)

Everyone will recognize the haunting opening of Beethoven's *Symphony No. 5*. It was used as the signal to the Resistance movement by the British during the Second World War and subsequently became famous as the introduction to '*Roll Over Beethoven*', brilliantly arranged and performed by Jeff Lynne and his Electric Light Orchestra in the seventies. Most people, too, leave school knowing one thing about Beethoven – that he was deaf. He's portrayed in the music-history books as something of a tempestuous, moody creative genius and this really isn't far off the mark.

He was born in Bonn in 1770 – again, from a musical family – and showed an enormous talent very early on. Like Mozart's father, Beethoven senior was quick to spot this and sought to exploit his son's gift at every possible opportunity. Family life was not without its troubles. His mother was for a time an alcoholic and his father, too, suffered with the same problem during the latter part of his life. This made its mark on the young Beethoven and undoubtedly played a part in developing his own highly charged, emotionally dramatic style of music and may have had some bearing on the fact that he, too, later developed a drink problem.

Beethoven had little formal education to speak of and was left with only very basic skills in reading and writing. There's a school of thought that suggests that Beethoven's profound ill temper could largely have been due to his inner sense of embarrassment and frustration at not being able to express himself very clearly and this may well have been the case. He did, however, have a very good musical training and quickly became proficient on a number of instruments including the piano, organ, violin and viola. In addition to a number of fine teachers that he had in Bonn, Beethoven also went to Vienna in his late teens to study with Mozart and following the death of both his parents Beethoven ended up making a living both as a teacher and as a viola-player in orchestras and opera houses in and around Bonn. Thinking that it would be a good career move, he, too, went off to Vienna, possibly owing to an encounter with Haydn, who was very impressed with young Beethoven's work.

After a time, Beethoven settled down in Vienna and developed a very good reputation – both as a performer and as a composer. Although from something of a lowly social background, he eventually started to move in the highest circles and received patronage and wrote works on commission for distinguished members of the aristocracy. He was quite prolific and wrote nine great symphonies, five brilliant piano concertos, as well as a whole host of chamber music, piano music and songs.

Beethoven's deafness manifested itself in about 1802, when he was just over thirty-two years of age. It didn't seem in any way to slow down his creative output even though he was also dogged by severe ill health for much of this middle to late period of his life. Rumour had it that Beethoven's deafness was due to the effects of syphilis and alcoholism. These ideas were dispelled only a matter of twenty years ago and popular belief now is that he had some kind of mysterious viral disease. The syphilis theory may have developed from the undoubted fact that Beethoven had countless affairs, mainly with married women from the ranks of the aristocracy. Whatever the disease, it can only have fuelled his frustration and loneliness, and must have contributed to his volatile, rather bitter nature.

Beethoven's ill health stayed with him for many years and by 1827 he was totally bedridden, suffering from pleurisy, pneumonia and dropsy. He died on 27 March that year and is buried in Vienna.

If you are a lover of orchestral music, then the symphonies and piano concertos are all wonderful pieces and I have included a few of the most popular in the list of recommended listening. The piano sonatas vary from being very easy on the ear to extremely challenging and intellectually stimulating. As a rule of thumb, the higher the opus number and consequently the later the work, the more complex his power of expression became. The string quartets are well worth listening to and from the chamber music that he wrote I have a particular favourite in the *Septet Op. 20*, which I highly recommend.

RECOMMENDED LISTENING

Symphony No. 5 Op. 67 (O)
Piano Concerto Op. 73 ('Emperor') (O)
Piano Sonata No. 14 Op. 27 No. 2 ('Moonlight') (I)
'Ode to Joy' from Symphony No. 9 Op. 125 (V/O)
Septet Op. 20 (Ch)

FURTHER LISTENING

Symphonies Nos. 3 and 4, Op. 55 and 60 (O)
Piano Sonata No. 23 Op. 57 ('Appassionata') (I)
Piano Trio No. 7 Op. 97 ('Archduke') (Ch)
Serenade for Flute, Violin and Viola Op. 97 (Ch)
Piano Sonata No. 31 Op. 110 in A flat (I)

Franz Schubert (1797–1828)

One of Schubert's most famous pieces was his *Symphony No. 8* ('*Unfinished*') and a few years ago there was an amusing television commercial featuring Schubert being persuaded to go out with his friends for a drink – the point being that he was unable to complete his eighth symphony because he couldn't resist the temptation of Heineken lager! It's a nice idea, but one that does not quite ring true, as the accepted reason for his being unable to finish the piece was that he, like Beethoven as it was supposed, had syphilis and was taken into hospital. He later staged something of a recovery and went on to write a number of other pieces, but sadly never got round to finishing off the piece that's made him famous the world over. Like

Mozart, however, Schubert did not have a long career and died of typhoid in 1828 aged only thirty-one.

Schubert's father was a teacher by profession, but also a very keen amateur musician and taught his son to play the violin from an early age. Franz was one of eleven children, of whom only three survived beyond infancy and his elder brother Ignaz taught him to play the piano. It seems that young Franz was a very bright child and excelled at everything he turned his hand to. Although aware of the exceptional talent that his son showed, his father insisted that Franz should get a 'proper job' and attend a teachers' training college. Franz reluctantly agreed and this led to his eventually accepting a job as a teacher alongside his father, although very much against his wishes.

However, the composer in him was not to be suppressed and Schubert was throughout this time continually writing music. In 1814 he wrote perhaps his first great masterpiece, which is now one of his most famous songs, '*Gretchen am Spinnrade*'. He was incredibly prolific at this time and in the following year, 1815, he wrote five operas (none of which is much good) and an astonishing 150 songs (pretty well all of which are fantastic).

Schubert was, as I have said, an extraordinarily bright child and his intellectual gifts stayed with him. He was an excellent improviser and would often entertain at soirées, social gatherings and dinner-parties by composing on the spot and playing music to dance to. This is a rare gift and one that he used to his further advantage by being able to remember what he'd played and subsequently writing it down. This explains how he built such a vast catalogue of music in his tragically short thirty-one years on this earth. He spent most of his life in and around Vienna and loved the very active social life that he led. He held appointments in many courts of the aristocracy and was a very popular man socially, always being invited out to dine with friends and colleagues.

He developed syphilis in 1822, could not finish the illustrious *Symphony No. 8* and then spent a rather miserable six years in and out of hospital until his death in 1828. He never really recovered from the disease and also suffered acute depression before contracting the typhoid which finally killed him. During these last five or six years of ill health he wrote some of his finest and most well-loved works including the *'Great' Symphony in C major,* the *Octet in F* (for string quintet, clarinet, bassoon and horn) and the song cycles *Die Schöne Müllerin, Schwanengesang* and *Die Winterreise.* Although he'd been an extremely popular man, he was quickly forgotten and it is only in the last hundred years or so that both he and his work have been valued alongside the other great classical Viennese composers, Mozart, Haydn and Beethoven.

Recommended Listening

Symphony No. 8 ('Unfinished') (O)
Piano Quintet in A ('Trout') (Ch)
Die Winterreise (V)
Octet in F (Ch)
Symphony No. 5 in B flat (O)

Further Listening

Symphony No. 9 in C major ('Great') (O)
Shepherd on the Rock (V/Ch)
String Quintet in C major (Ch)
Ballet music Rosamunde (O)
Die Schöne Müllerin (V)

Felix Mendelssohn (1809–47)

The opening to Mendelssohn's *Violin Concerto* has a beautifully lyrical understated romanticism about it that makes it among the most popular of all concertos for any instrument. Mendelssohn only lived for a mere thirty-eight years, but during that very short time he composed a significant number of the enduring classical favourites, including the *Wedding March* from *A Midsummer Night's Dream*, the *Hebrides Overture* (*'Fingal's Cave'*) and the *Violin Concerto*, all of which are regularly performed in concert halls around the world.

Felix Mendelssohn was the son of a wealthy banker and received a very high-powered education from the finest teachers in Paris and Berlin, including the poet Goethe. His mother, Lea, taught him the rudiments of music and he was soon hailed as being 'another Mozart'. The talent he demonstrated both on the piano and as a composer and improviser certainly drew a close comparison between the two. His talents were developed by an immense amount of hard work and application: His father insisted on his getting up at five o'clock every morning to start work.

He composed his now famous *Octet* for double string quartet at just sixteen years of age – a miraculous achievement – and the following year produced the overture to *A Midsummer Night's Dream*. Not satisfied, however, with just a career as a composer, Mendelssohn studied philosophy at the University of Berlin and continued in his search for knowledge, all the while mixing in the highest academic and artistic circles, becoming friends with the poet Heine and later with other composers like Chopin and Robert Schumann.

He came to England in the spring of 1829 and Sir Walter Scott took him on a voyage to Scotland and the Hebrides, where he found the inspiration for the overture of the same name. From this time he was composing some very fine music and by 1833 he had completed four symphonies, a couple of string quartets and the first volume of *Songs without Words* for solo piano. He was naturally prolific and his music has a youthful spontaneity and freshness about it quite unlike any other composer of his generation.

Mendelssohn was also keen on conducting and travelled all over the world working with many of the finest orchestras in performances of his own works and those of others that he admired, including pieces by Bach, Handel and Beethoven. While in France in 1837 he married a beautiful young French girl, ten years his junior. They had five children and the strain of this, coupled with his intensely busy schedule as a conductor and composer, led to his poor health. He was always under par and was reputed to have been a pretty sickly sort of chap.

His music found favour with the Prussian and British royal families and he very much enjoyed giving royal performances at Buckingham Palace in London and for Frederick Wilhelm IV in Berlin. He wrote a lot of piano music – a couple of concertos and four volumes of the *Songs without Words* – and, apart from the symphonies and the famous overtures, he also wrote two excellent oratorios: *St Paul* in 1836 and *Elijah* ten years later. It was following a splendid performance of *Elijah* in Berlin that he returned to Leipzig suffering from complete exhaustion. He had a series of fits and died on 4 November 1847.

His music displays the unique qualities of warmth and romanticism while at the same time retaining the clarity of texture and tunefulness of the early classicists. His music is really very appealing and is now finding something of a resurgence in popularity.

Don't be confused by seeing the name Bartholdy added to Mendelssohn's surname: It was the name adopted by his father when he abandoned Jewry and some publishers retained the use of the full double-barrelled surname.

Recommended Listening

Violin Concerto in E minor Op. 64 (O)
Incidental music to A Midsummer Night's Dream (O)
Symphony No. 4 ('Italian') (O)
Hebrides Overture (O)
Octet for Strings Op. 20 (Ch)

Symphony No. 3 ('Scottish') (O)
Elijah (Or)
Piano Concerto No. 2 in D minor (O)
Songs without Words Nos. 1–48 (I)
Prelude and Fugue Op. 35 No. 1 (I)

The Strauss Family

Nineteenth-century Vienna was hailed as the capital city of dance music owing to the efforts of the Strauss family. Johann the elder was the son of an innkeeper but quickly became a prominent figure, leading his own orchestras in cafés, ballrooms and dance halls and writing and arranging all his own music. After a few years his repertoire added up to more than two hundred dances, a hundred and fifty of which were waltzes.

Johann had three sons who all followed in his footsteps, the most famous of whom was 'Johann II' who wrote such enduring favourites as *'The Blue Danube'*, *'Tales from the Vienna Woods'*, *'Die Fledermaus'* and the ever popular *'Emperor Waltz'*. The other two brothers were less famous but equally active in the world of music, with Josef writing *'Music of the Spheres'* and *'Dynamiden'*, both of which are frequently performed today, while Eduard made more of a name as a conductor.

The music from the Strauss family is probably the most popular light classical music in the repertoire – audiences love it and there are frequently concerts dedicated solely to performances of these works, the most famous being the televised New Year's Day concert live from Vienna.

As well as the waltzes already listed, the family were renowned for writing marches and polkas, the most famous of these being Johann Strauss senior's *'Radetzky March'* and Johann Strauss II's *'Pizzicato Polka'*.

Recommended Listening

'Tales from the Vienna Woods' (O)
Die Fledermaus (Op)
'The Blue Danube' (O)
'Emperor Waltz' (O)
'Thunder and Lightning Polka' (O)
'Radetzky March' (O)
The Gypsy Baron (Op)
'Tritsch-Tratsch' (O)
'Music of the Spheres' (O)
'Dynamiden' (O)

Where to Go from Here in the Classical Style

Mozart, Haydn, Beethoven and Schubert between them wrote a vast amount of music, most of which is brilliant and is well worth exploring if you are a fan of classical music in general. You could go for anything by any of these composers and not be disappointed, although I obviously feel that the pieces I have recommended in the lists are the ones that really shouldn't be missed. Some late Beethoven can be a bit more challenging than his earlier works and it is worth bearing this in mind if you wish to explore on your own or if you're looking at the programmes of concerts that you may be interested in actually attending.

I have selected three other composers of the day that are also well worth investigating: J. C. Bach (son of JS), Ludwig Spohr and Carl Maria von Weber.

Recommended Listening

J. C. Bach:
Orione (Op); *Piano Concertos Nos. 1–40* (O)
Ludwig Spohr:
Clarinet Concerto No. 1 in C minor Op. 26 (O); *Nonet Op. 31* (Ch)
Carl Maria Von Weber:
Konzertstück Op. 79 (O); *Overture to Euryanthe* (O)

Other lesser-known composers whose works you may well also wish to explore include:

LUIGI CHERUBINI
CARL MARIA VON DITTERSDORF
DOMENICA CIMAROSA
CHRISTOPH WILLIBALD GLUCK

THE ROMANTIC PERIOD

Romantic music strikes a chord with most of us although some may find it too sugary and emotional for their own taste. Rachmaninov and Tchaikovsky are among my favourites and if you've seen the film *Brief Encounter* you will immediately identify with the highly charged score by Rachmaninov.

Johannes Brahms (1833–97)

Brahms was another composer whose talents were recognized very early in life. His father was a musician, playing the french horn in the militia band in Hamburg and the double bass in ad-hoc groups that were performing in taverns and at various social functions in and around the city. The first musical training young Brahms received was in the form of piano lessons and already by the age of ten he was showing signs of possessing an extraordinary talent. An American impresario who was in Hamburg at the time was very taken with him and immediately proposed a big tour of the United States, but this was wisely refused by his teacher. Responsibility for Brahms' future development and tuition was then handed over to the highly respected Eduard Marxsen, who later became his mentor.

Brahms left school at the age of fifteen in order to get out and earn some money. He did occasional concerts but also worked for publishers arranging popular music of the day. In 1853, when he was twenty, the Hungarian violinist Eduard Remenyi offered him the opportunity of a tour giving concerts together and this proved to be the big turning-point in Brahms' career. Through meeting up with various celebrated musicians like Joachim and Franz Liszt, Brahms eventually met Robert and Clara Schumann. Robert Schumann was someone whom Brahms held in the highest regard and Schumann's wife Clara was also a gifted concert pianist. They both loved Brahms' work and soon became his close friends. Robert Schumann did not have a stable constitution and his mental breakdown in 1854 came as no surprise to those who knew him well. Brahms showed his deep concern for the Schumann family and he was at Clara's side throughout this very difficult period in her life. When Robert Schumann eventually died in 1856, Brahms made it known that he was very much in love with Clara, but although the bond was never to be broken they decided not to spend their lives together. This had a significant effect on Brahms' music. In nearly all of the pieces from this time on, there is quite clearly a mood of heartfelt emotional yearning, giving the works an intensity that has rarely been equalled by other composers.

His career, with its occasional ups and downs, was very successful. He eventually settled in Vienna where he established a fine reputation both as a conductor of the great classical masterpieces and as a composer. The works that really established him on the international scene were the *German Requiem* and the *Alto Rhapsody*. He then went on to write the four symphonies, two piano concertos and a marvellous collection of chamber music, piano pieces and songs. Brahms became quite a rich man in his later years and, although he was not one to flaunt his wealth, he very much enjoyed the good life – holidays in villas throughout Europe with celebrated friends and acquaintances, smoking expensive cigars and eating well to help maintain his portly image.

He had a tendency to find very young girls attractive and at one time was deeply smitten with the Schumanns' third daughter, Julie, although it was quite obvious that he was never going to forget his former love, Clara. Clara died in 1896 and, while this did not come as a great shock to Brahms, he was deeply affected by her death. His own health deteriorated and on seeking medical advice he learnt that he had advanced cancer of the liver. He died just one year later under exactly the same circumstances as that of his father.

Brahms has become one of the best-loved composers of romantic music. All of his works are beautifully crafted – from the piano miniatures and songs to the extravagantly architectured symphonies and great choral works. For me, the most endearing aspect of his music is the lovely reflective, autumnal quality to the later chamber music and the works listed below really shouldn't be missed. Also, with Brahms, I would suggest more than one hearing. The first time I heard the *Clarinet Quintet Op. 115*, I couldn't really make sense of it, but the more I listened, the more I grew to love it, now finding that as a single piece of music it encapsulates so many feelings and emotions that I can directly relate to.

Recommended Listening

Symphony No. 1 (O)
The German Requiem (V/O)
Piano Concerto No. 2 (O)
Clarinet Quintet in B minor Op. 115 (Ch)
Four Ballades Op. 10 (I)

Further Listening

Symphonies Nos. 2, 3 and 4 (O)
The Academic Festival Overture (O)
The Horn Trio Op. 47 (Ch)
The Hungarian Dances (O)
Romanzen und Lieder Op. 84 (V)

Peter Ilyich Tchaikovsky (1840–93)

If you see a concert advertised as a 'Tchaikovsky Night', you can expect two things: First, that you will hear the *1812 Overture*, the *Piano Concerto No. 1*, *Romeo and Juliet* or *Swan Lake* and quite probably one of the *Symphonies Nos. 4, 5 and 6*, with perhaps a bit of the *Nutcracker Suite* thrown in for good measure; second, that the concert hall will undoubtedly be full because these really are all great works that have found a place in the hearts of audiences all around the world ever since they were written. Tchaikovsky's style is marked by wonderful tunes, luscious harmonies and dramatic colourful orchestrations and if you are a lover of mainstream classical music, then this is quite probably the music for you.

Tchaikovsky was rather strange as a young boy and, it seems, became even stranger as time went on. There was a piano in the house where he was born and his parents were somewhat taken aback to hear him being able to play on this piano the tunes that he'd heard and become familiar with on their St Petersburg music-box. They sent him off for formal piano lessons and with such an exceptional ear for music he naturally made fantastic progress straight away. However, the family were suffering great difficulties at this time. Tchaikovsky's father had problems with his job and it was necessary to send Peter and his brother to a boarding school. This had a profound effect on Peter, which was compounded by the death of his mother (from cholera) shortly after the family had found security again in St Petersburg in 1854.

Tchaikovsky never really found his direction and ended up as a clerk in the Ministry of Justice. Having always been a man of slightly odd habits, he was known to be partial to chewing up official documents – an activity that was not well received by his colleagues. He eventually left this rather formal occupation in search of enjoyment and satisfaction in pursuing a career in music; and, having such an extraordinary talent, success was not long in coming and he soon found himself a respectable job at the Moscow Conservatoire.

Having kicked the habit of chewing documents, Tchaikovsky then suffered all sorts of physical and mental problems including hallucinations, hypochondria, colitis and tingling sensations in his extremities. Nevertheless he continued his work and wrote some wonderful (and some not so wonderful) music. The early symphonies are generally regarded as pieces of little stature, but works like *Swan Lake, Romeo and Juliet,* the *1812 Overture* and the *Symphonies Nos. 4, 5 and 6* have become all-time favourites.

Tchaikovsky was homosexual but always had in the back of his mind a desire to get married. He did so in 1877, to an attractive but very odd girl by the name of Antonina Milyukova who was apparently a nymphomaniac and thought she had the power to bring Tchaikovsky round. However, after just five days Tchaikovsky wrote a letter to his brother saying 'physically she is totally repulsive to me!' and of course things went from bad to worse. He ended up running away to his sister's estate at Kamenka and made an unsuccessful attempt to take his own life.

It was at this point that another woman entered his life who this time was to be his saviour: Nadezhda von Meck, a very wealthy widow who was extremely fond of music. She looked after Tchaikovsky by giving him an annual allowance of six thousand roubles, but it appears that the two hardly ever met in person, preferring to correspond in lengthy explicit letters to each other. In 1896, Tchaikovsky's wife Antonina died tragically in a lunatic asylum (to which she had been committed owing to her sexual derangement) and his relationship with Madame von Meck seemed to provide all he needed from a relationship with someone of the opposite sex: security, understanding and affection without any physical contact. This all went towards helping him find his creative genius once more, and he was moved to write the opera *Eugene Onegin* and the *Symphony No. 4* in 1878.

Following a break in the relationship with Madame von Meck and the death of his father, Tchaikovsky spent his last twelve years as something of a nomad. He lived mainly in hotels and was a man of extreme habits. He would always wake at seven in the morning, have a cup of tea and then read the Bible. At 9.30 precisely he would begin composing and then spend the afternoons walking, using the evening for yet more composing and proof-reading. It was not until about 1888 that he really started to compose anything of great note (the early part of the decade had been a bit bleak) but with the *Symphony No. 5*, his symphonic poem *Hamlet* and the wonderful ballet score for *Sleeping Beauty* Tchaikovsky was at his most inspired. In 1893 he wrote the work that he considered to be his finest, the *Symphony No. 6* (*'Pathetic'*). Tchaikovsky admitted to having found writing it an intense and emotional experience, being frequently moved to tears while composing. It was given a strangely cool reception in St Petersburg, which I suppose is not surprising as it really is a work of extraordinary vision that needs more than one hearing fully to appreciate it. In November of the same year he foolishly drank a glass of water straight from the tap, knowing full well that it was the middle of the cholera season. He died four days later in tragic circumstances on 6 November 1893.

In certain highbrow circles, Tchaikovsky's music is looked down upon for being over indulgent and too obvious in its expression – the very reasons that it is among the most popular of all music the world over. Much of the music would be ideal as the soundtrack for films and the main theme from the *Fantasy Overture 'Romeo and Juliet'* has been used on television for all kinds of commercials and romantic background music. If you do see a concert advertising the music of Tchaikovsky, do try it and keep in mind all the troubles and the inner problems he faced throughout his life. You will find it a moving and enjoyable experience.

Recommended Listening

Fantasy Overture 'Romeo and Juliet' (O)
Swan Lake (O)
Serenade for Strings (O)
Symphony No. 6 ('Pathétique') (O)
1812 Overture (O)

Further Listening

Symphony No. 4 (O)
Piano Concerto No. 1 and Violin Concerto (O)
Variations on a Rococo Theme for Cello (O)
Hamlet (O)
Eugene Onegin (Op)

Robert Schumann (1810–56)

Schumann is depicted as being a dreamy, totally impractical artist who would be the archetypal representative of the Romantic Movement. He was born into a very wealthy family and his father was a bookseller and publisher. Not surprisingly, young Schumann had an avid interest in the literary world, an interest that really started at school where he was totally absorbed in both books and music. He was already composing quite a lot of music at this time, mainly piano music and these early works show the wonderful youthful spontaneity that he later lost.

New medical evidence suggests that quite early on in his life he contracted syphilis (yes, another one!), the mercury treatment for which may have led to his right hand becoming crippled. Another theory for this affliction is that he was overworking his hands in the pursuit of technical piano practice; but, whatever the reason, the result was that his career as a concert pianist was terminated, to be instantly replaced by his career as a composer. He wrote a large number of works in a very short space of time and many of these pieces are now among the standard repertoire of today's concert pianists. He also developed his skills as a writer about music and he is renowned for his outspoken but usually well informed critical judgements on the music and art of the day.

Wieck, his teacher, had a beautiful daughter, Clara, with whom Schumann fell in love. When Clara's father found out about the affair he was furious and forbade his daughter to marry. The situation became acrimonious to the point where Robert Schumann brought a lawsuit against Wieck forbidding him to interfere any further in their relationship. Robert and Clara were married in 1840 and this turbulent episode is undoubtedly typical of Schumann's passion and pursuit of romantic notions. Clara was very good for Schumann; she was a loyal and excellent critic of his work, always encouraging and supportive of his endeavours. She encouraged him to write symphonies, something that he had always yearned to do as he considered the symphony to be the real 'truth' in music.

After a few years, however, things took a turn for the worse and Schumann placed extraordinary constraints on his wife, claiming that he needed absolute silence while composing. This caused a problem as Clara was herself one of the leading concert pianists of the day and needed to practise. These and other problems eventually led to Schumann suffering a nervous breakdown and terrible hallucinations which may well have been due to the effects of his syphilis. They decided after a time that life was becoming too stressful, so Schumann left his job at the Leipzig Conservatoire and the couple moved to Dresden in search of peace and quiet. A few years passed and then Schumann decided to take up another job in Düsseldorf. This also turned out to be a disaster and only made his mental and emotional problems worse. Throughout this time he'd struck up friendships with a number of other famous composers of the day including Mendelssohn, Wagner and later the young Brahms. However, following some particularly severe bouts of depression and hallucinations, Schumann threw himself into the Rhine in an attempt to commit suicide. He was unsuccessful and was sent to a mental asylum in Bonn, where he spent the last few years of his life.

He has left us, however, with a lot of great music, especially in the fields of piano music and song. It is also widely accepted that he made a truly significant contribution to the development of *lieder* (German songs) – establishing the piano as an equal partner to the voice, not simply as the accompaniment.

Recommended Listening

Carnival (I)
Symphony No. 4 in D minor Op. 120 (O)
Dichterliebe (V)
Piano Trio in D minor Op. 63 (Ch)
Piano Concerto in A minor Op. 54 (O)

Further Listening

Papillons Op. 2 (I)
Fantasia in C Op. 17 (I)
Symphony No. 3 in E flat ('Rhenish') (O)
Konzertstück for Four Horns and Orchestra (O)
Frauenliebe und Leben Op. 42 (V)

Frédéric Chopin (1810–49)

Both Chopin and Liszt were astounding virtuoso pianists and their works now provide the backbone of the repertoire for concert pianists wishing to perform music from the Romantic Movement. Following a period in Victorian times when their music was regarded as being sugary and too sentimental by half, they are now held in high regard and enjoyment of their works is world wide.

Chopin was always fascinated by music and took up the piano, quickly becoming proficient enough to be hailed as a *Wunderkind* (child prodigy) at the age of sixteen. He took a great interest in the folk music of the day and this features strongly in nearly all of the music he wrote. He went to study at the famous Warsaw Conservatoire and by the time he was nineteen had already composed a large catalogue of piano music – nocturnes, polonaises, waltzes and the two concertos for piano and orchestra. Following visits to Western Europe and the personal dilemma of whether or not he should return to his native Poland, he eventually decided in 1831 to settle in Paris. Life was hard and he was desperately short of money, barely scraping a living. He did, however, eventually find favour with the Rothschild family, who frequently employed him to play at soirées and this opened up a new circle of wealthy people who also wished to employ Chopin to give lessons at their houses. During this time he was constantly composing and added to his already quite extensive catalogue of concert pieces, including nocturnes, mazurkas and the popular *Ballade No. 1 in G minor*.

Chopin was always dogged by ill health and, following his meeting the *femme fatale* George Sand, he agreed to go away with her and her children to the island of Majorca. It was here that Chopin was suspected of contracting tuberculosis and because of this they were evicted from their rented accommodation and had to stay in a rather damp and unwelcoming disused monastery. He was deeply depressed at this time and was moved to compose the now famous funeral march which he used as the slow movement in the piano sonata that he was writing at the time. His condition deteriorated and they all had to pack up and travel to Marseilles where fortunately he received excellent medical attention that apparently saved his life.

Following an almost complete recovery, Chopin, George Sand and the children went back to Paris, but in order to avoid society gossip Chopin and George Sand decided to live in separate flats very near each other.

Chopin undertook a series of private recitals (at very high fees), took on a few talented pupils and life started to take a turn for the better. He was not only prolific but also writing very fine music.

However, in 1847 domestic troubles reared their ugly head once more and, following a particularly bad spate of arguments with George, the couple finally decided to go their separate ways. Chopin eventually went to England but was not happy there and it became increasingly apparent that his creative muse had dried up once and for all. He wrote in a letter to a friend that he felt 'played out' and 'incapable of bringing forth new sounds' – a sad state of affairs lasting some eleven months until his death. His funeral was held at the Madeleine in Paris where, at his own request, Mozart's *Requiem* was sung.

Recommended Listening

Nocturne in E flat Op. 9 No. 2 (I)
Ballade No. 1 in G minor Op. 23 (I)
Polonaise in A major Op. 40 No. 1 (I)
Scherzo in B flat minor Op. 31 (I)
Berceuse Op. 57 (I)

Further Listening

Twenty-four Preludes Op. 28 and the Nocturnes 1–21 (I)
Études Op. 10 and Op. 25 (I)
Waltzes Nos. 1–14 and Mazurkas 1–51 (I)
Sonata in B flat minor Op. 35 (I)
The Cello Sonata (I)

Franz Liszt (1811–86)

Franz Liszt was universally renowned for being the most gifted pianist in the world and his formidable technique led him to write fiendishly difficult music. Chopin was, it appears, quite disparaging of Liszt's talents and is quoted as saying that 'He is an excellent binder who puts other people's works between the covers'. There is an element of truth in this remark as Liszt was a prodigious arranger of other composers' works, eventually producing some nine hundred transcriptions. At the time that he wrote them he was also about the only person who could actually perform them. However, it is now accepted that he, too, was a composer of some fine music in his own right and he holds a high-ranking position in the field of romantic piano music.

The story of Liszt's life makes very interesting reading. One of the main themes that keeps recurring in all the historybooks is that he was blessed with remarkable sexual athleticism. He lived for a long time with a countess who was the mother of his children, one of whom later went on to marry the celebrated opera-composer Richard Wagner. Liszt had a following all over Europe not dissimilar to the sort of adulation and fanaticism attached to the pop stars of the sixties and tales of his sexual exploits are rife.

When he was just eleven years old, the family moved to Vienna where he was placed with two of the finest tutors of the day: Czerny for lessons in piano and Mozart's rival Salieri for composition. As a youngster, Liszt gave successful concerts in Vienna and his talent and work were admired by Beethoven and Schubert among others, who agreed with the popular notion that Liszt was a young prodigy following in the footsteps of Mozart – quite an accolade! Liszt was constantly in demand as a concert pianist and he spent many years travelling around Europe delighting audiences wherever he went.

Throughout this whole time he was always soul-searching and trying to come to terms with his spirituality. He had been brought up with a strong church background and his father had at one time been a Franciscan novice for two years. However, his religious upbringing did not stop him living with his lover, the Countess Marie d'Agouli and having children out of wedlock. They finally separated in 1844 and following this break-up Liszt took the children to live with his mother in Paris. Career-wise this was a time of enormous success for Liszt and in 1847 he met a lady who very nearly made him settle down for good. This was the Princess Carolyne Sayn-Wittgenstein whom he had met in Kiev. She persuaded him to stop touring and concentrate on a more stable career as a composer. This he duly did, with spectacular results, writing what are now regarded as some of his finest compositions. He spent most of his time in Weimar and stayed there until the tragic deaths of his son Daniel (aged only twenty) and his daughter Blandine (aged twenty-eight).

It was at this time that he finally felt the urge to get married – this time to the Princess of Rome. Sadly the marriage was not to come to fruition as the Pope denied her the right to divorce from her existing husband. Liszt then became heavily involved with the Church again and even went as far as taking the four minor orders of the Catholic Church, while all the time concentrating on writing religious music. However, he never actually became a priest and spent his last years giving master classes on the piano and advising and teaching up-and-coming composers of the day among whom were Borodin, Fauré, Saint-Saëns and Debussy.

Liszt had a greater talent for writing for the orchestra than Chopin and he was actually the first to develop the symphonic poem – an extended one-movement piece of music depicting a story or a painting, for example. He was also the first to give a complete concert of solo piano music – now called a piano recital. He was quite rightly hailed as one of the finest keyboard virtuosos ever to have lived, not only performing his own works but also pioneering some of the great works of his predecessors Bach, Beethoven and Schubert.

Recommended Listening

Piano Concertos Nos. 1 and 2 (O)
Hungarian Rhapsodies for Orchestra Nos. 1–6, G. 359 (O)
Les Préludes (O)
Liebesträume Nos. 1–3, G. 541 (I)
Funerailles, G. 173/7 (I)

Further Listening

Études d'exécution transcendante, G. 139 (I)
Mephisto Waltz No. 1, G. 514 (I)
Six Consolations, G. 172 (I)
Verdi's Rigoletto, G. 434 (I)
Piano Sonata in B minor, G. 174 (I)

Sergei Rachmaninov (1873–1943)

Imagine the steamy scene on the station platform in the classic film *Brief Encounter* and hear in your mind the evocative music that so heightened that emotional moment. It was Rachmaninov's *Piano Concerto No. 2*, one of the most popular pieces of all time and essential (to coin the record industry's current buzz-word) to your collection. It's a brilliant example of music from the Romantic period and ranks among Rachmaninov's greatest triumphs.

He was born into an aristocratic family on the estate of Oneg, between Leningrad and Moscow, but the family's fortunes were declining and when Rachmaninov was nine the estate was sold and his parents split up. Sergei was the fifth of six children and showed exceptional talent very early, probably inherited from his father who was also an excellent pianist. Rachmaninov was sent to the St Petersburg Conservatoire in 1883 at just ten years of age, but only stayed for a couple of years, moving on to the celebrated Moscow Conservatoire to study with Sverev. Sverev was a master pianist and a highly respected teacher who was a strict disciplinarian. He insisted that his pupils lived with him, so that he could supervise their overall development and take them to concerts and the opera, giving them the chance to mingle with the artistic celebrities of the day. Rachmaninov shared a room with another boy and they took turns with the piano in their room, on which they had to practise in three-hour stretches. Sverev omitted to encourage Rachmaninov's undoubted talent as a composer and this appears to be the one glaring failing in his otherwise meticulous and highly productive method of instruction.

After attending a summer school for students of advanced harmony and composition, Rachmaninov composed a study in F sharp minor for piano. Sverev was so impressed with the piece that he played it to Tchaikovsky, who was also taken by the work. This led to Rachmaninov taking formal lessons in composition. These proved unsuccessful and, after falling out with both his composition teacher and Sverev, Rachmaninov decided to leave the conservatoire a year early. He passed his final exams with honours and was awarded a gold medal for composition. Sverev was at the presentation ceremony and, despite their falling-out, he was so delighted to see his young protégé receiving such an accolade that he gave him his own gold watch, a memento that Rachmaninov was to treasure for the rest of his life.

Rachmaninov didn't have an easy life. He had moderate successes as a composer, but none of these provided him with any kind of stable income to fund a secure base from which to work. As well as accompanying and teaching (which he loathed) he set to work on a symphony which received its first performance in 1897 conducted by Glazunov (another Russian composer). The performance was a complete disaster. Not only was it one of his weaker pieces; it also received a second-rate performance. Rachmaninov realized this and went into a severe depression, only to be brought out some months later by a wealthy friend who provided him with the opportunity of a conductorship at the Moscow Opera House.

The move to Moscow so inspired Rachmaninov that he started to do very good work again but, following a trip to England where he received wonderful reviews for his tone poem *The Rock* and the now famous *Piano Prelude in C sharp*, he returned to Russia and immediately slipped back into his depression. A psychologist named Dahl helped him out of this phase by a form of auto-suggestion using the phrase 'You are going to start writing, and it will be excellent'. It worked. Rachmaninov went on to complete the *Piano Concerto No. 2*, got married and had two lovely children.

His life then seemed to be a relatively happy mixture of work as composer, conductor and concert pianist. He has been hailed as probably one of the finest pianists since Liszt and we are fortunate to have recordings of him performing his own works in the current catalogues. Rachmaninov and his family moved around quite a lot during the following years, settling in the United States in 1918 and in Switzerland in 1931. The last thirty or so years of his life were spent mainly as a concert pianist as he was finding composition more and more difficult. He was struck down with cancer in his early forties and he died one month after his last recital on 28 March 1943. He is buried in the Kensico Cemetery in New York.

He is the natural successor to Tchaikovsky in the Russian Romantic Music school and while pointing you enthusiastically towards the *Piano Concertos Nos. 2 and 3*, the *Symphony No. 2* and a few of the *Preludes*, I can highly recommend a closer look at many of his other works.

Recommended Listening

Piano Concerto No. 2 (O)
Piano Concerto No. 3 (O)
The Piano Preludes (I)
Rhapsody on a Theme by Paganini (O)
Symphony No. 2 (O)

Further Listening

The Rock (O)
The Bells (O)
The Isle of the Dead (O)
The Cello Sonata (Ch)
Vesper Mass (V)

Gustav Mahler (1860–1911)

The son of an ambitious father who had made his way out of humble origins, Gustav Mahler gave a piano recital at the age of ten which caused a sensation in the town of Iglau in Bohemia. He was another child prodigy and, following this concert, was sent off to the conservatoire in Vienna to begin a formal training in music. There he was an outstanding student and received all kinds of prizes and awards. This naturally pleased his father very much for it was he who was the ambitious driving force of the family.

Mahler's childhood was marred by the constant rowing and unsettled relationship between his parents; and this in turn later had a profound effect on his music. We know that he was an extremely sensitive being and that his music is quite often autobiographical in nature. Most of his works portray aspects of his character and feelings or are musical pictures of specific events in his life. He was an intense and astutely aware person who appears very much to have been 'an old soul', showing a wisdom and clarity of vision that was truly exceptional. His music very clearly depicts human emotions and the sounds of nature as well as reflecting his extraordinary awareness of death.

Mahler was regarded as being a bit of an oddball. He was a strict vegan and only consumed water, fruit and spinach! This was unusual at the end of the nineteenth century and people that came in contact with him were taken aback by the man's rather peculiar habits. Although extremely successful as a student, when Mahler failed to win the coveted Beethoven Prize (and consequently the cash that went with it) he decided to concentrate on a career as a conductor, feeling that there was more chance of commercial success in that direction. All the while, however, he continued to compose and public performances of his works were held in high regard. He became a much sought after composer and graduated to writing for the full symphony orchestra. His *Symphony No. 1*, written in 1888 when he was just twenty-eight years old, is a masterpiece that is now firmly placed in the repertoire of every major orchestra around the world.

His talent as a conductor was unquestioned and he was always in demand. Tchaikovsky once wrote of him that he was 'undoubtedly a genius and a man of extraordinary ability'. Brahms, too, was unfailing in his praise of Mahler and he is quoted as saying: 'To hear the true *Don Giovanni* – go to Budapest.' This is where Mahler was the resident conductor and he was receiving rave reviews for all his performances of Mozart, Puccini and Verdi operas. Mahler also conducted the first performance of Tchaikovsky's *Eugene Onegin*. It seems that there was only one person of note who was not an admirer of Mahler and this was the famous conductor and pianist Hans von Bülow. Von Bülow was a close friend and a professional colleague of Brahms and Wagner, but dismissed Mahler's offerings in one classic sentence, 'If this is still music, I know nothing of music,' and he was to be the bane of Mahler's life for some time. Von Bülow's death in 1894 gave Mahler a new creative lease of life and a greater freedom to express himself and have his works performed.

While composing Mahler required absolute silence and even went to the lengths of writing in solitude in a hut near Steinbach, where he would insist on the cows being stripped of their bells, farmers curtailing their activities and animals either being cooped up or sent far away so as not to disturb him. Steinbach and his summer house in Toblach were ideal settings for one so sensitive and inspired works that have a natural and spiritual quality to them.

Mahler fell in love with a girl called Alma Maria Schindler, the step-daughter of the artist Carl Moll and married her in 1902. This was not an easy relationship by any means as Mahler was a man of extraordinary habits and had something of a dictatorial nature. He made his wife, also a highly talented musician, give up composition and he demanded total freedom for himself so that Alma should serve his every need. This obsessive, somewhat selfish pursuit of excellence was the hallmark of his life – always seeking the truth and demanding the very best from everyone around him.

He left Vienna in 1907 after a ten-year reign at the opera house. This was also the year in which his eldest daughter died and Mahler was found to have a chronic heart condition, reputedly a hereditary problem from which his mother had also suffered and died. While staying in Schluderbach he became fascinated by a collection of Chinese poems and these inspired him to write the wonderful song-cycle *Das Lied von der Erde*, which some would say is his finest creation. His last few years were overshadowed by an awareness of impending death and, having been taken seriously ill in New York in 1911, he moved back to Paris where he died. Mahler specified that there should be no memorial to him and that he should be allowed to pass over quietly to a new life. In the last few days of his life he is quoted as saying, 'Tomorrow we shall run faster, stretch out our arms and one fine morning . . .' thus confirming his firm religious belief that death is most certainly not the end. His wife has beautifully encapsulated her last thoughts in the following: 'I can never forget his dying hours and the greatness of his face as death drew nearer. His battle for eternal values, his elevation above trivial things and his unflinching devotion to truth are an example of his saintly life.'

While getting to know the works of Mahler, an insight into the life and spirit of the man himself helps to give a far greater appreciation of the music. Listen to any of the symphonies and particularly the highly emotive song '*Abschied*' ('*Farewell*') from *Das Lied von der Erde*, of which Mahler genuinely asked: 'Can this be endured? Will people not kill themselves afterwards . . . ?'

Recommended Listening

Symphony No. 5 (O)
Symphony No. 1 (O)
Symphony No. 4 (O/V)
Das Lied von der Erde (V/O)
Kindertotenlieder (V/O)

Further Listening

Symphony No. 8 (O/V)
Lieder eines fahrenden Gesellen (V/O)
Symphony No. 2 (O/V)
Des Knaben Wunderhorn (V/O)
Symphony No. 9 (O)
Symphony No. 6 (O)

Richard Strauss (1864–1949)

Almost without exception, everyone will recognize the music from the film *2001: A Space Odyssey*. It is a classic movie theme tune and has a dramatic intensity that has captured the imagination of the public the world over. Richard Strauss was said to be the last of the great German Romantics. He epitomizes the true spirit of the Romantic composers and while others around him were experimenting and moving away from the traditions that had been set before them Strauss developed from where Brahms and Schumann had left off. He successfully combines the elements of drama, intensity and apocalyptic beauty in his music, while still adhering to the essential principles of writing melody, harmony and rhythm in a conventional way, unlike most of his contemporaries. This is gripping music and, although much of it was written only forty or fifty years ago, is music to which we can all relate today.

Strauss was born into a highly musical family. His father was an exceptional horn-player and started Richard's piano lessons when his son was only four. Young Richard began to compose just two years later, with some considerable degree of success – there was an obvious talent here. He was a bright young man who sailed through school and university, eventually studying philosophy and aesthetics alongside music. He was a tall good-looking figure, who very much dressed the part of a businessman and in his later years it is common knowledge that he would only undertake conducting engagements if the money was right!

His career started when a connection was made with the celebrated Hans von Bülow, with whom it seems nearly all the eminent Romantic composers came in contact at one time or another. This association led to his being offered a succession of jobs in Munich where he met his wife Pauline, a singer from the Munich Opera. He quickly developed a reputation as a marvellous conductor and was very much in demand right up until the end of his days.

However, like most other composers, the first performances of his compositions invariably provoked extreme reactions and this was obviously something that deeply upset and angered Strauss at the time. He is now, of course, looked upon with some degree of reverence, particularly for his tone poems that demonstrate a remarkable gift for writing for the orchestra in a vivid, colourful and exciting way. He was also very keen on writing operas and among his triumphs in this field are *Der Rosenkavalier*, *Salome*, *Elektra* and *Arabella*. Throughout the period of his life when he was at his most prolific he held a succession of prime jobs in Berlin and Vienna and was never one to be forced into doing things against his will. This led inevitably to his being involved in a number of difficult situations, but by and large he managed to find ways around such problems, only leaving one post acrimoniously – that of the directorship of the Vienna Opera, from which he resigned in 1924.

His earlier works and those written in the last four or five years of his life are the ones that demonstrate his best creative output and they really are well worth exploring for lovers of colourful, exciting, highly charged late Romantic music.

Recommended Listening

Also Sprach Zarathustra (*2001* theme) (O)
Till Eulenspiegel (O)
Don Juan (O)
Four Last Songs (V/O)
Der Rosenkavalier (Op)
Horn Concerto No. 2 (O)

Further Listening

Ein Heldenleben (O)
Metamorphosen for Twenty-three Solo Strings (O)
Le Bourgeois Gentilhomme (O)
Alpine Symphony (O)
Oboe Concerto (O)
Elektra (Op)

Where to Go from Here in the Romantic Style

The music of the composers included in this section on the Romantic period is, I think, comprehensively the most appealing. If you wish to explore further, then other composers to turn to include Bruckner, Reger and Bruch. Lovers of opera also have an enormous catalogue of music to enjoy, including the works of Verdi, Wagner and Puccini.

French Music

French music has a very distinctive quality to it, ranging from the ethereal sounds of the Impressionists (Debussy, Ravel and others) to the passionate dramatic music of Berlioz in his *Symphonie fantastique*.

Hector Berlioz (1803–69)

Berlioz has for many years been portrayed as being something of a wild, passionate, mysterious Frenchman whose music has never really been understood. He is most famous for his *Symphonie fantastique*, but he did write a number of other very fine works that can be heard both on the concert platform and on record.

As a boy, Berlioz showed a keen interest in music and while his parents were keen for him to have piano lessons he preferred the flute and the guitar and became quite proficient on both these instruments. His father was a doctor and was responsible for his son's education, which is why the boy was never really given the encouragement to pursue a career in music. Instead he was bundled off to medical school in Paris very much under sufferance. He positively disliked studying medicine and after falling out with his parents on a number of occasions eventually entered the Paris Conservatoire to follow his interest in music.

He was a man of great determination and set his sights high in wanting to win the coveted Prix de Rome. This he achieved in 1830. He loved going to the opera, concerts and plays and it was during a visit to the theatre that he first saw the young actress Harriet Smithson with whom he fell in love. They married in 1833.

Harriet was the source of much inspiration for Berlioz, in particular for his famous work the *Symphonie fantastique* which was first performed in December 1829. Berlioz was immensely proud of this work and commented that the piece was 'entirely autobiographical in intent'. It is one of the most famous examples of programme music, incorporating all kinds of emotion and scenes within the piece including macabre visions of witchcraft, passion and pastoral reveries.

In contrast to this work, the great violin virtuoso of the day, Paganini (also a fine viola-player) commissioned Berlioz to write a piece for viola and orchestra. This he did, although Paganini was not greatly impressed with the result, to the point of not even wanting to play the solo part in the first performance. Today viola players are delighted to have the four-movement work, *Harold in Italy*, in their repertoire.

In his lifetime Berlioz never really achieved much success, which is why he was never comfortably off. His operas *Benvenuto Cellini* and *Les Troyens* were failures, as was *La Damnation de Faust*, a concert work that is occasionally staged. He is now remembered for a handful of truly excellent pieces and for being a wonderfully romantic idealist who did actually influence other composers through his radical approach to composition, both formally and orchestrally.

Recommended Listening

Symphonie fantastique (O)
Overture Le Corsaire (O)
Romeo and Juliet (O)
L'Enfance du Christ (Or)
Harold in Italy (O)

Further Listening

Overture King Lear (O)
Les Nuits d'été (V/O)
Overture Le Carnival Romain (O)
Les Troyens (Op)
La Damnation de Faust (O)

Gabriel Fauré (1845–1924)

Fauré is best-known for one work in particular, his *Requiem*, which is regularly performed all over the world. He is also famous for a tune within the *Pavane* for chorus with orchestra. This piece is invariably to be found in compilation albums of popular classical favourites.

He was born into a largish family, one of six children and having little contact with his parents was looked after by the nanny. Fauré's talent for music became apparent very early on and he was given a free place at a special music school in Paris where he was taught by another eminent French composer, Camille Saint-Saëns. He excelled at his studies and started writing music in a very original style, showing a remarkable talent for composing for the human voice and it is in this medium that he really excelled.

He was a very gifted organist and held a number of prestigious jobs in Paris, once being the assistant to Widor (whose *Toccata* is the most popular music played at the end of weddings in Britain). The piano was his other favourite instrument and he composed two wonderful quartets for violin, viola, cello and piano in 1879 and 1886 respectively. These are among the most charming pieces in the whole chamber music catalogue for this combination. One or two of his solo works for piano have also found their way into the repertoire of many concert pianists and these include the *Barcarolles* and *Nocturne*, while his collections of songs contain so many gems that it is hard to know which to mention. Popular favourites include *'Nell'*, *'Les Berceaux'* and *'Claire de lune'*.

In 1896, Fauré was appointed chief organist at the Madeleine and also a professor of composition at the Paris Conservatoire. He is reputed to have been a fine teacher and was instrumental in developing the talents of Ravel, Schmitt and Nadia Boulanger among others. He was promoted to director of the conservatoire some years later, a job which carried mixed blessings as this gave him less time for his own composition.

Sadly Fauré went deaf in 1910 and for the last fourteen years of his life this was a severe handicap, having a marked effect on his music. Much of the work from this period is very sombre, bare and transparent in texture and requires sympathetic performance. He died in 1924 but has left us with the most beautiful collection of music that ensures his place as one of the truly great French composers of the late nineteenth century, paving the way for the prodigious talents of Debussy and Ravel.

Recommended Listening

Requiem (V/O)
Pelléas et Mélisande (Op)
Pavane (V/O)
Piano Quartet No. 1 in C minor Op. 15 (Ch)
Les Berceaux (V)

Further Listening

Élégie (I)
Barcarolle (I)
Ballade (I/O)
Cinq Mélodies (V)
Dolly Suite (I)

The French Impressionists

The school of composers known as the French Impressionists includes Debussy and Ravel, supported by Roussel, Ibert and Dukas. They are naturally linked with the nineteenth century pictorial Impressionists, Monet, Manet, Seurat, Pissaro, Renoir, Cézanne and others. Debussy is hailed as the 'founder' of the French Impressionist school of composers (an accolade which he loathed) and his music, alongside that of Ravel, ranks among the most popular on the concert platform today.

The *Prélude à l'après-midi d'un faune* is one of the most celebrated works from this period, while Ravel's *Bolero* is another great example of a piece that has achieved cult status following its inclusion in the Dudley Moore and Bo Derek film *10* and as the soundtrack to Torville and Dean's ice-skating triumphs in 1987.

Debussy and Ravel set the trend for avoiding the formal, dramatic, direct means of expression employed by their predecessors, in favour of using 'colours of sound' and textures to create shimmering atmospheres. This was the perfect foil to what the French painters had achieved, using subtle shades and textures coupled with innovative use of light. Even without listening to the music, some of the titles give direct clues as to the style: *Reflets dans l'eau (Reflections in the Water), Nuages (Clouds), La Mer (The Sea)* and *Cloches à travers les feuilles (Bells Heard through the Leaves)* for example.

Claude Debussy (1862–1918)

Debussy was born in Paris and was something of a child prodigy. He came from humble origins, the son of a shopkeeper, but was obviously given great encouragement by his parents, starting piano lessons at the age of seven and going on to study at the celebrated Paris Conservatoire from the age of twelve. Ten years later he won the coveted Prix de Rome, which enabled him to spend a number of years in quiet isolation writing at the Villa Medici in Rome. Debussy's life was generally troublesome, particularly in his relationships with women: His wife, Lilly Texler, attempted suicide when he left her for another woman and following their divorce in 1904 Debussy was plagued by ill health, most particularly with cancer of the rectum.

He was an absolute master of orchestration and his music never fails to conjure up vivid images in the listener's mind. Much of the music is deemed to be programmatic – musical representation of a picture, a poem, a story – and obvious examples are to be found in *La Mer* and *Nuages*, where the music is unmistakably conjuring images of the sea and of clouds sweeping across the sky.

Debussy loved the music of Wagner and so it is curious that this did not inspire him to write more than a couple of operatic works of which *Pelléas et Mélisande* is the most famous. Debussy is best known for his wonderful orchestral works, the piano music and superb collections of songs. Small wonder that he is regarded as perhaps being the most influential of all twentieth-century composers.

Recommended Listening

Prélude à l'après-midi d'un faune (O)
La Mer (O)
Nocturnes (O)
Reflets dans l'eau (I)
Chansons de Bilitis (V)

Further Listening

String Quartet (Ch)
Trio for Flute, Harp and Viola (Ch)
Pelléas et Mélisande (Op)
Pour le piano (I)
Première Rhapsodie for Clarinet and Orchestra (O)

Maurice Ravel (1875–1937)

Like Debussy, Ravel was brought up in Paris and studied at the Paris Conservatoire. After a few years he joined the composition class of the eminent composer Gabriel Fauré. Ravel was greatly prolific and has left us with a fine collection of orchestral, piano, vocal and chamber music. He, too, had problems in his lifetime. He served in an ambulance corps at the front in the First World War, but was demobilized owing to ill health in 1917. Following a serious car accident in 1935, he suffered from an unusual kind of mental paralysis and died two years later after an unsuccessful operation on his brain.

His experiences made him a man of nervous disposition and he was consistently plagued by insomnia. He was a great socialite and enjoyed being in the company of friends, never happier than when sitting around drinking in bars and cafés. He loved both gourmet and simple French cooking and meals would always be followed by strong French cigarettes.

Debussy was a great admirer of Ravel's talent and once said of him that he 'possessed the finest ear that ever existed'. Much of Ravel's music is more direct and immediately 'dramatic' in style than that of Debussy. Listen to *Bolero* or *La Valse* for an extraordinary display of Ravel's skill in writing for the orchestra; better still, go and hear them performed live in the concert hall and you will experience a truly spectacular event.

Both Debussy and Ravel wrote a great deal of music for the piano and if you are a fan of that instrument and you're keen on this evocative French style of music, then you will find a rich catalogue of varied music from each. Ravel's *Gaspard de la nuit* and *Miroirs* are quite remarkable and are frequently heard on the concert platform today. They also both wrote one great string quartet each and lovers of chamber music will not be disappointed. Among my personal favourites is the *Introduction and Allegro* for flute, harp, clarinet and string quartet and it must rank as being one of the finest examples of French Impressionistic chamber music in the catalogue.

Ravel had to work hard to achieve the recognition he deserved. In many ways his music is very forward-looking and he, like Debussy, has been the source of much inspiration for many composers who have followed.

Recommended Listening

Bolero (O)
Introduction and Allegro (Ch)
Daphnis and Chloë Suites 1 and 2 (O)
Pavane pour une infante défunte (O and I)
La Valse (O)

Further Listening

String Quartet (Ch)
Miroirs (I)
Alborado del gracioso (O and I)
Trois Poèmes de Stéphane Mallarmé (V/Ch)
Shéhérazade (V/O)

Where to Go from Here in the French Style

DUKAS:
The Sorcerer's Apprentice (O); *Ariane et Barbe-bleue* (Op)
IBERT:
Escales (O); *Trois Pièces Brèves* (Ch)
ROUSSEL:
Evocations (O); *Sérénade* (Ch)
GOUNOD:
Petite Symphonie (Ch); *Faust* (Op)
SAINT-SAËNS:
Organ Symphony No. 3 (O); *Carnival of the Animals* (O)
POULENC:
Piano Concerto (O); *Organ Concerto* (O); *Gloria* (V/O); *Trio for Oboe, Bassoon and Piano* (Ch)
MILHAUD:
Suite provençale (O); *Suite française* (O)
SATIE:
Trois Gymnopédies (I); *Trois Gnossiennes* (I); *Trois Morceaux en forme de poire* (I)
FRANCK (Belgian!):
Symphony in D minor (O); *Sonatas for Cello and Violin* (I); *Symphonic Variations* (O)

English Music

The music written by English composers from the middle of the nineteenth century is, by and large, easily identified and has an unmistakably 'English' quality to it. Perhaps the best example is Elgar's *Pomp and Circumstance March No. 1*, otherwise known as *'Land of Hope and Glory'*. The very mention of this piece instantly conjures up a picture of the Last Night of the Proms, banners waving and everyone feeling extremely nationalistic and proud to be British. Some would say that it should be the national anthem.

Composers like Frederick Delius, Ralph Vaughan Williams, Gustav Holst and Gerald Finzi also have this distinctive quality to their music, which is usually quite grand, full of rich modal harmonies and lyrical tunes which perfectly capture the spirit of the English character and countryside. When you know a little bit about these composers, this comes as no surprise. Most of them were around during Edwardian times and were naturally affected by the strongly patriotic mood of the day. Many of them were lovers of the countryside, spending much of their lives in either the Cotswolds, the Malvern Hills or the Yorkshire Dales. These influences undoubtedly show through their music and you only have to listen to any snippet of a work by Elgar or Vaughan Williams to get a pretty clear picture of what characterizes English music from this period.

Edward Elgar (1857–1934)

Elgar was born near Worcester in 1857 and died there in 1934. He came from a very musical family and his father was an organist who also owned the local music shop. Growing up in such a strong musical environment, it's not surprising that young Edward Elgar quickly became proficient at playing a whole range of instruments including the piano, violin, cello and double bass, as well as the bassoon and the trombone. What is surprising, though, is that for the most part Elgar was largely self-taught. It was not until later that his true quality as a composer began to emerge, following a lengthy period when he made a living as a teacher, as a violinist and as the bandmaster to the staff of a lunatic asylum.

Elgar was an ambitious man and tried to make a career in London but failed and moved back to his former home in Worcester, where he decided to concentrate on his work as a composer. He wrote a number of works for choral societies in the area which were performed at festivals throughout Britain and finally his big break came in 1899 when he composed the *'Enigma' Variations*. This was enormously well received and established his reputation as one of the finest British composers – an accolade that has remained to this day.

Elgar had a marvellous gift for writing for string instruments and his Concertos for violin and cello have been among the top-selling classical recordings for many years. Nigel Kennedy's award-winning recording of the *Violin Concerto* may well, in time, match the popularity of Jacqueline du Pré's historic recording of the *Cello Concerto*, conducted by Sir John Barbirolli.

In addition to his greatest large-scale masterpieces, Elgar did write a number of shorter works for string orchestra that are no less enjoyable and are definitely well worth exploring. They are very often to be found on recordings as compilations.

Recommended Listening

'Enigma' Variations Op. 36 (O)
Cello Concerto in E minor Op. 85 (O)
Violin Concerto in B minor Op. 61 (O)
The Dream of Gerontius (V/O)
Introduction and Allegro (O)

Further Listening

Serenade for Strings (O)
Chanson du matin and Chanson de nuit (O)
The Elegy (O)
Sospiri (O)
The Apostles (V/O)

Frederick Delius (1862–1934)

Delius was an extraordinary character. Born into a very wealthy family, he was the son of a highly successful Prussian industrialist who had settled in Bradford. Young Delius rebelled against his father's wishes for him to follow in his footsteps and ended up running an orange plantation in Florida.

His time in the United States had a great effect on him and it was while travelling down a river one summer evening that he heard some negroes singing in close harmony and was inspired to write music himself. He had lessons with someone locally, whom Delius claimed taught him more in three months than he learnt in three years in Leipzig where he later settled. Delius was a truly cosmopolitan character, travelling the world throughout his life, collecting the influences of different cultures that went to make up his own style – something of a cross between the best of both the English and French schools of composers who were writing at the time. He lived for a while in Scandinavia and also in France and Germany, frequently visiting England for performances of his works, many of which were championed by the great conductor Sir Thomas Beecham.

His music is largely rhapsodic in nature; some would say it has no form, but for his devotees that is exactly what is attractive about it. Always dreamy, colourful and atmospheric, this is music that has also proved to be influential. Delius had a sense of harmony that was very much his own and his orchestrations produce wonderfully evocative textures that have blatantly been copied by today's composers of film scores. He wrote beautifully for the orchestra and also had a good degree of success with writing for the voice, while his other works include sonatas and concertos for violin and cello as well as many songs.

Recommended Listening

On Hearing the First Cuckoo in Spring (O)
Summer Night on the River (O)
Brigg Fair (O)
In a Summer Garden (O)
Appalachia (O)

Further Listening

Cello Concerto (O)
Violin Sonata (I)
A Mass of Life (V)
Sea Drift (Or)
Fennimore and Gerda (Op)

Ralph Vaughan Williams (1872–1958)

Vaughan Williams was introduced to music from a very early age, with his mother and aunt encouraging him to learn the organ, piano and violin. They also enrolled him for a correspondence course in the theory of music – this all happened by the time he was nine! He was born into a very well connected family and his father was a clergyman who sadly died when young Ralph was only three.

By the age of fifteen he had already decided that he was going to be a composer and this was at the forefront of his mind throughout his whole time at Charterhouse School. He went on to study with Sir Hubert Parry (composer of '*Jerusalem*') at the Royal College of Music and on finishing his course there decided to continue to study at Trinity College, Cambridge. Ever striving for more knowledge, he went back to the Royal College and worked with Charles Stanford (another respected English composer) and later to Berlin to study with Max Bruch. This was not enough for Vaughan Williams and he ended up having a course of lessons from the French composer Maurice Ravel.

Vaughan Williams had no financial worries and was able to pursue these activities under relaxed and unpressured circumstances. However, he took a highly professional attitude to his work and composed some very fine music. He was much acclaimed all over the world and went down particularly well in the United States of America where he was hailed as the 'Grandfather of English Music'. The symphonies are perhaps his best-known pieces and, like Beethoven, he wrote nine, two of which stand out above the rest: *No. 2* ('*London*') and *No. 3* ('*Pastoral*'). He also had an avid interest in folk-song and hymns, which led to his revising the English Hymnal in 1906. Much of his work is based upon traditional folk-song ideas and this characterizes the music as being quintessentially English.

Recommended Listening

Symphony No. 2 ('London') (O)
Symphony No. 3 ('Pastoral') (O)
The Lark Ascending (O)
Fantasia on a Theme by Thomas Tallis (O)
Songs of Travel (V/O)

Further Listening

Sinfonia Antartica (O)
The Wasps Overture (O)
Fantasia on 'Greensleeves' (O)
Oboe Concerto (O)
Flos Campi (V/O)

William Walton (1902–83)

Born in Lancashire, Walton won a place as a chorister at Christ Church, Oxford and left at the age of sixteen having already gained his degree. While he was there he made a number of acquaintances who were to become very influential in his career, most importantly Sacheverell Sitwell.

Walton lived with the Sitwell family for some time and derived enormous benefit from the cross-cultural exposure that he was subjected to. The Sitwells introduced him to Constant Lambert, a much respected composer of the day who played a significant part in influencing Walton's own style of composition.

The Sitwells devised a special piece of home entertainment in the form of a work entitled *Façade*: Poems by Edith Sitwell were set to music by Walton, arranged for a small diverse collection of instruments shielded from the audience by a curtain through which a megaphone was inserted for the narration of the poems. From the unlikely drawing-room setting of the first performance, this has now probably become Walton's most famous piece and the aptly titled '*Popular Song*' is a tune that many will know as the signature tune to the always popular BBC television programme 'Face the Music', hosted by Joseph Cooper.

Walton went through an intensely creative period following the success of *Façade* and produced such fine works as the overture *Portsmouth Point*, the *Viola Concerto* and *Belshazzar's Feast*. In 1935 came the *Symphony No. 1*, which is still regarded as one of the most important symphonic works written by a British composer during the interwar years. He then found a new outlet for his work in the form of film music and wrote the scores to a number of famous films including *Henry V*, *Hamlet* and *Richard III* – all three stemming from a fruitful collaboration with Laurence Olivier.

After the war, Walton's music lost something of its former glory and sense of inspiration. He had, during this period, moved to Italy and this may have had something to do with the inherent change in style. However, the opera *Troilus and Cressida* is a fine work, although not often now performed.

Walton once said of himself that he was 'a classical composer with a strong feeling for lyricism' and this is definitely the case. The works recommended in the listening-lists are all well worth exploring if you are a fan of British music in general.

Recommended Listening

Crown Imperial (O)
Façade (V/Ch)
Viola Concerto (O)
Symphony No. 1 (O)
Belshazzar's Feast (V/O)

Further Listening

Portsmouth Point (O)
String Quartet (Ch)
Henry V (film music) (O)
Troilus and Cressida (Op)
Escape Me Never (film music) (O)

Benjamin Britten (1913–76)

Benjamin Britten is probably the most outstanding British composer this century. He had a unique voice in the world of composition and has left us with a catalogue of works, many of which are already considered masterpieces and will find themselves in the standard classical repertoire for ever more.

Britten was something of a child prodigy. By the time he had left his prep school, he'd already composed more than forty works. He met up with Frank Bridge, who advised him to go and study at the Royal College of Music with John Ireland. Britten did not enjoy his time at the college very much and only ever heard one of his works performed while he was there. The year after he left college, he joined the GPO Film Unit where he stayed for five years. He was responsible for providing the music soundtracks for films and while there made some very useful contacts, including the poet W. H. Auden, with whom he later struck up a close relationship both professionally and personally.

Britten consistently produced fine works throughout his life. One of the early high points in his career was to perform his own *Piano Concerto* at the Proms in 1937. However, he got itchy feet and he and his closest friend Peter Pears the tenor set off for Canada, later settling in Long Island in the United States. They returned in 1942 and Britten continued to write, quickly making a name for himself composing opera. The first real triumph was *Peter Grimes*, which is now regarded as a classic. This was followed by *The Rape of Lucretia* (for eight singers and twelve instrumentalists) and *Albert Herring*, another full-scale masterpiece.

Britten moved house from Snape to nearby Aldeburgh in Suffolk where he and Peter Pears set up their own festival in 1948. This has since become a much-loved annual event and ranks alongside the major international festivals presenting music and artists of the highest calibre.

Prolific by nature, Britten has left us with a startling array of works in many forms – operas, orchestral music, songs, instrumental works and concertos. He also struck up a friendship with the celebrated cellist Rostropovich; this inspired the wonderful *Suites for Unaccompanied Cello* written between 1965 and 1971 as well as the lesser-known *Symphony for Cello and Orchestra (1963)*.

Britten died in 1976 following heart trouble, having made his mark as one of the finest twentieth-century composers. In particular, his artistry in writing for the voice demonstrates a dramatic simplicity that can be appreciated by everyone.

Recommended Listening

Serenade for Tenor, Horn and Strings (V/O)
Albert Herring (Op)
Variations on a Theme of Frank Bridge (O)
Phaedra (V)
Solo Cello Suite No. 1 (I)

Further Listening

Sinfonia da Requiem (V/O)
War Requiem (V/O)
Peter Grimes (Op)
Violin Concerto (O)
Hymn to St Cecilia (V/O)

Michael Tippett (b. 1905)

Tippett's music has only recently found a place in the hearts of music-lovers the world over. This is for a number of reasons, perhaps the first of which is that his music is by its very nature not immediately accessible to the casual listener. He writes in a style all of his own, often using flourishes of notes that can sound cluttered and clumsy in the wrong hands. When performed well, however, it becomes atmospheric and inspired, with an intensity not unlike the music of Benjamin Britten.

Tippett was born in London but spent much of his early years abroad as his family lived for long periods in the south of France, in Corsica and in Florence. He went to the Royal College of Music when he was only seventeen and studied composition with Charles Wood, while also having conducting lessons with two of Britain's most distinguished maestros, Sir Adrian Boult and Sir Malcolm Sargent.

Tippett's career didn't really take off until he was about thirty. His earlier works were not of much substance and the first pieces he was satisfied with were the *String Quartet No. 1* and the *Sonata for Piano (1937)*. The Second World War interrupted his career in two ways. Firstly by the general fact that musical life was disrupted with orchestras, concert halls and publishing houses all being directly affected by the war. Secondly because, as a conscientious objector refusing to do any approved war work, he was sentenced to three months' imprisonment for not complying with his conditional exemption.

However, the war did prove to be a source of inspiration and he wrote an oratorio entitled *A Child of Our Time* that was performed in 1944. It is a marvellous work that makes a very strong protest at the inhumane persecution that was going on at the time. Tippett wrote the libretto himself, having sought the advice of T. S. Eliot, whom he had initially approached to write the text. Eliot was so impressed by Tippett's initial drafts that he recommended him to continue alone, which is exactly what he did.

Following this troubled period in his life, things progressed well, with an abundance of commissions and plenty of inspiration bringing forth operas, string quartets, piano sonatas, symphonies, concertos and various other works for more esoteric combinations of instruments, often including the voice. Sir Michael is truly one of this country's finest composers, who has not only expressed himself in a unique way but has also maintained a caring interest in all aspects of social problems throughout the world and reflected them in his writing.

Recommended Listening

A Child of Our Time (Or)
The Midsummer Marriage (Op)
Songs for Dov (V/O)
The Sonata for Four Horns (Ch)
Fantasia Concertante on a Theme of Corelli (O)

FURTHER LISTENING

The Ice Break (Op)
Symphony No. 4 (O)
Concerto for Orchestra (1963) (O)
Suite in D (O)
Piano Sonata No. 3 (I)

Where to Go from Here in the English Style

There is a wealth of English music to find out about and if you enjoy the general style and flavour of this rich, tuneful, harmonic music, then other composers and their works that you should now go on to include: Gerald Finzi, Gustav Holst and Sir Hubert Parry.

RECOMMENDED LISTENING

FINZI:
Clarinet Concerto (O); *Grand Fantasia and Toccata* (O); *The Ode to St Cecilia* (V/O); *Dies Natalis* (V/O); *Intimations of Immortality* (V/O)
HOLST:
The Planets (O); *The Choral Symphony* (V/O)
PARRY:
'Jerusalem' (V/O); *'Blest Pair of Sirens'* (V/O)

NATIONALISTIC MUSIC

Every country has produced its own unique sound and here follows a look at the famous composers from the countries that have produced the most distinguished nationalistic music over the last few centuries. I have not included much on the music from Spain as by and large this particular national school is confined to the works of literally just a handful of composers who wrote mainly for the piano or the classical guitar. There are, however, one or two composers who have produced some good orchestral music – like Rodrigo, whose *Concerto de Aranjuez* (for guitar and orchestra) even entered the pop charts! Without being disparaging of other Spanish composers, Rodrigo is really the 'main man' and, while also not wishing to be disparaging about him, the *Concerto de Aranjuez* is definitely the piece to look out for!

Leos Janáček (1854–1928)

A much underrated composer, Janáček ranks among the greatest of creative forces ever to have emerged from Czechoslovakia. Rather oddly he wrote nothing of any great consequence until in his sixties, but from that point on he never looked back. His music has an incredible rhythmic vitality about it, while at times being hauntingly romantic. Janáček was fascinated by Czechoslovakian folk culture and this proved to be a tremendous source of inspiration which is clearly reflected in his music.

He was one of fourteen children and by all accounts a bright child whose talent for music was recognized by his father quite early on. His family were not well off and they sent young Leos off to the monastery school where there was a talented teacher of music from whom Janáček was to gain a very good grounding. He eventually decided to train as a music teacher and ended up teaching at the monastery school where he had been a pupil. Not surprisingly, being a teacher didn't provide the creative stimulus for which he yearned; and this is evident in his early compositions, which are, in the main, pretty dull and lacking in any kind of character. Janáček was well aware of this and had the necessary self-motivation to get some money together and head off for Prague where he did a crash course at the Organ School in search of knowledge and inspiration. He left after a year with an impressive set of qualifications and then moved around various respected seats of learning, always in the back of his mind wishing that he could start his own music college.

He had rather radical and, at the time, unconventional theories about music – for instance that music should follow speech rhythms and also relate to birdsong. He felt passionately about this and these theories proved not to be quite as strange as they may at first have seemed. A number of composers since have modelled their works in this way with quite beautiful results – listen to Messiaen's *Oiseaux exotiques* for a stunning example of birdsong translated into music.

Time rolled on and Janáček failed to make any significant impact on the music business, all the while pursuing his interest in speech rhythms and nationalistic folk music. His big break finally came in 1916 when the National Opera in Prague agreed to stage his opera *Jenufa*. It was a complete success and before long the opera was being performed all over Europe. In the remaining twelve years of his life he then went on to write perhaps a dozen really excellent pieces, a mixture of operas, choral, solo and chamber music. At the age of sixty-four, while still married, he fell deeply in love with another woman and she played a significant role in inspiring the old man to compose probably his finest works – one of which is the string quartet appropriately entitled *'Intimate Letters'*.

Recommended Listening

Sinfonietta (O)
'Intimate Letters' String Quartet No. 2 (Ch)
Jenufa (Op)
Glagolitic Mass (V)

Further Listening

Mladi (Ch)
The Cunning Little Vixen (Op)
From the House of the Dead (Op)
Taras Bulba (Op)

Bedrich Smetana (1824–88)

Like Beethoven, poor old Smetana was deaf for much of his life and for the last few years he was absolutely stone deaf. Tinnitus, a common complaint these days for people who have subjected their ears to sustained loud music, was also another of Smetana's afflictions and – again, like Beethoven – he was troubled by an incessant high-pitched whining noise in his head.

This was not to deter the composer from writing music that is splendidly colourful, drawing on the folk idiom from his native land. Much of his music is overtly nationalistic in character. Listen to his set of symphonic poems *Ma Vlast (My Country)*, one of which ('*Vltava*') depicts a musical journey down the river towards the sea.

Smetana is known as the father of Czech music and he came from an intensely musical family. There's a story that he took part in a performance of a Haydn string quartet at five years old and then gave his first piano recital just a year later! He was an ambitious but lazy young man and a good example of his desire to be famous is to be found in a well-known entry in his diary that boldly states: 'I wish to become a Mozart in composition and a Liszt in technique.'

His earlier works did not receive a very good response; but, never to be worn down or dejected, he made it his business to try to get in with the right people. He made contact with Berlioz, Robert and Clara Schumann and on one occasion even wrote to Liszt enclosing a set of piano pieces dedicated to his hero – at the same time asking for a loan. Liszt proffered some good advice and tried to help him find a publisher, but tactfully chose to ignore the pleas for money. Undeterred, Smetana decided to open up his own music school in Prague, in search of recognition and fulfilment, neither of which he achieved, owing to the unstable political climate – particularly for musicians, who mainly made their way to Paris or Vienna.

A succession of jobs followed, including one in Sweden during which time he got married and had four children of whom, sadly, only one was to survive. His wife, Katerina, died young from tuberculosis and Smetana soon remarried and in 1861 moved back to Prague. His life followed a somewhat troubled course, with mixed reactions to his compositions. Plagued by his terrible deafness, he died in a mental asylum at the age of sixty suffering from syphilis.

His music is now recognized as being some of the finest to have emerged from Czechoslovakia and lovers of Slavonic folk-style music will find much to enjoy here.

Recommended Listening

Ma Vlast (O)
From Bohemia's Fields and Forests (O)
The Bartered Bride (Op)
Six Characteristic Pieces for Piano (I)
String Quartet No. 1 (Ch)

Further Listening

The Two Widows (Op)
The Kiss (Op)
String Quartet No. 2 (Ch)
Piano Trio (Ch)
The Secret (Op)

Antonin Dvořák (1841–1904)

Cast your mind back to a steep cobbled hill somewhere in Yorkshire; imagine the smell of freshly baked brown bread and hear in your mind the gentle sound of the brass band playing the slow movement of Dvořák's *'New World' Symphony*. It's the Hovis commercial of course and, while it was not quite what Dvořák had in mind, I'm sure he would have been deeply touched by such a sensitive treatment of his great masterpiece.

Dvořák is the foremost Czech composer. His music ranks with that of the great writers of the nineteenth century, being performed by orchestras in concert halls all over the world. He was held in high regard by a number of other eminent composers. Tchaikovsky was a friend and admirer and Brahms was once moved to write: 'I should be glad if something occurred to me as a main idea that occurs to Dvořák only by the way!' Dvořák had a very special talent for writing beautiful tunes and his works are littered with great melodies that sound so spontaneous you can't help but have them ringing in your ears long after the music has stopped.

He's another one who started music at a very early age and, like the other great composers, showed enormous promise straight away. He got jobs as a viola-player in various orchestras, notably the Czech National Opera Orchestra and was often conducted by one of his heroes: Smetana. It was here that he got his own first inspirations to write opera and working alongside Smetana was undoubtedly of great benefit. He was also obsessed with the works of Wagner and, having made contact with the maestro, is reputed to have attended every single performance of Wagner's work at the German Theatre in Prague. His own forays into the world of composing were not received with the wildest enthusiasm, but this did not deter him and he continued to write symphonies, string quartets and song cycles until, in the mid-1870s, no-one could ignore him any longer. Brahms had long championed his works and had helped Dvořák's career by getting him a publishing deal. Dvořák won the Austrian State Prize four years running and finally made his mark with works like the *Serenade for Strings* and the now immensely popular *Slavonic Dances*.

It was from then on that Dvořák never looked back. He was invited all over the world both as a conductor and as a professor of music. He spent three years in the United States where he wrote his *Symphony No. 9 ('New World')*, but spent the last few years of his life in his native land in the city of Prague as the director of the conservatoire.

Recommended Listening

Symphony No. 9 ('New World') Op. 95 (O)
Slavonic Dances Op. 46 and Op. 72 (O)
Serenade for Strings in E Op. 22 (O)
Cello Concerto in B minor Op. 104 (O)
Dumky Piano Trio Op. 90 (Ch)

Further Listening

Symphony No. 7 Op. 70 (O)
Serenade for Wind Op. 44 (Ch)
Piano Quintet in A Op. 81 (Ch)
String Quartet in F Op. 96 ('American') (Ch)
Stabat Mater Op. 58 (V/O)

Béla Bartók (1881–1945)

Bartók stands out as the most famous composer to have emerged from Hungary. His style is very clearly derived from the folk music of his native land and characteristically combines wonderful folk tunes with energetic rhythms in a gypsy idiom.

Born near the borders of Hungary, Yugoslavia and Romania, Bartók was brought up by his mother, following the death of his father when the boy was only seven years old. It was a hard life: Young Bartók was always ill and his mother had to work to keep the family on an even keel financially.

The political climate at the time was most unsettled and this, too, placed its own restrictions on the early years in Bartók's life. He showed enormous promise as a musician and became the organist of the Gymnasium Chapel in Pozsony, later taking up a place at the Budapest Academy. He was offered a place at the celebrated Vienna Conservatoire, but turned this down in order to follow his first love: Hungarian folk music.

In 1905, Bartók teamed up with Kodály to carry out an in-depth survey of folk music from many countries including their own and this provided the main creative influence on their compositions thereafter. A few years later Bartók accepted a position as a professor at the academy where he had himself been a student and, following the First World War, he really began to produce works of considerable stature including the wonderful music to the ballets *The Wooden Prince* and *The Miraculous Mandarin*, as well as a whole host of piano pieces and a couple of string quartets.

Also a fantastic concert pianist, Bartók was attracting praise from all quarters and was awarded a special prize in the United States for his extraordinarily difficult work the *String Quartet No. 3*. Bartók travelled to America and to Britain on a number of occasions as a concert pianist and his works were invariably well received.

Bartók, however, was deeply affected by the political distractions around him and the depression he felt at seeing the growing Nazi control of central Europe shows through his work. He was an intensely proud man who desperately wanted to make his own way without the assistance of others wherever possible. He was also a withdrawn individual and this may have stemmed from the problems he had experienced as a child and through not having a father for the important years of his childhood. He married twice, each time to pupils who were both considerably younger than himself.

Care should be exercised when exploring the works of Bartók. His *Concerto for Orchestra* written in 1943 is a wonderful work that shows a masterly skill at writing for the orchestra and this is now often used by symphony orchestras around the world as something of a showpiece. The *Music for Strings, Percussion and Celesta* is also a very approachable work, as is the *Piano Concerto No. 3*. The *Dance Suite* and the *Romanian Dances* are essential listening which can lead one on nicely to the more astringent world of the string quartets and piano music.

Recommended Listening

Concerto for Orchestra (O)
Romanian Dances (I/O)
Piano Concerto No. 3 (O)
Music for Strings, Percussion and Celesta (O)
Viola Concerto (O)

Further Listening

Duke Bluebeard's Castle (Op)
The Miraculous Mandarin (O)
Dance Suite (I)
String Quartets Nos. 1–6 (Ch)
Two Rhapsodies for Violin and Piano (Ch)

Zoltán Kodály (1882-1967)

Kodály was an almost exact contemporary of his compatriot Bartók and in many ways their lives and music share similarities. They both worked very closely together on their collections of folk music and, like Bartók, Kodály incorporated many of these themes and influences in his works.

Kodály had an unsettled childhood, being moved around by his family, until at the age of eight he went to the Budapest Academy to study music. He was an outstanding student and his early compositions show a distinct reverence for Brahms, whose music he loved. Later on, following the close association with Bartók and the folk music collection, his own music became altogether more Hungarian in style and his first really great work came in 1925 with the suite from the opera *Hary Janos*, followed by the *Dances of Galanta* in 1933.

Kodály loved travelling and was a frequent visitor to Europe and the United States, all the while maintaining an active stance as a highly respected professor of music at the Academy in Budapest. However, just before the

Second World War he resigned from his job having earned the reputation as the most influential teacher ever to have worked in Hungary. His methods of teaching were adopted throughout the country and he had become something of a musical institution.

Only a handful of Kodály's works are regularly performed today, the two works mentioned above being the most popular. However, Kodály did have an extraordinary gift for writing music that is not only exciting to listen to but also exciting to watch. A marvellous example of this is the *Solo Sonata for Cello*, which is a real *tour de force* and should not be missed if you see it advertised in a concert programme. In a similar vein is the wonderful *Duo for Violin and Cello* that embodies similar characteristics. For the orchestra, he was never afraid to use unusual colours of sound within his orchestrations and especially interesting in the *Hary Janos Suite* is the use of the Hungarian instrument the cimbalom (a sort of harp or zither whose strings are struck with padded mallets). He also used the saxophone to great effect, another instrument neglected by many a classical composer.

Do give this music a try: It's terrific and would be a welcome addition to any classical collection.

Recommended Listening

Hary Janos Suite (O)
Dances of Galanta (O)
Solo Sonata for Cello (I)
The Spinning Room (Op)
String Quartets Nos. 1 and 2 (Ch)

Further Listening

Peacock Variations (I)
Psalmus Hungaricus (V)
Dances of Marosszek (O)
Hymn of Zrinyi (I)
Too Late (V)

Modeste Mussorgsky (1839–81)

Mussorgsky has been described as 'Russia's most individual and human musical genius' and it is a tragedy that his life should have been cut short by alcoholism at the relatively young age of forty-two.

Mussorgsky studied the piano from the age of five and showed considerable talent. Like many of the famous composers he gave a concert as a youngster that signalled the extraordinary talent that he possessed but, while everyone around him was aware of his gift, Mussorgsky chose to ignore it, disliking the idea of the hard work and discipline that would be required to bring it to fruition.

The family moved to St Petersburg when Mussorgsky was just ten years old. He was sent to the Military Academy and, although he showed a serious interest in early Russian church music, it seems that Mussorgsky was unable to concentrate on anything very much other than demolishing his liver by frequent bouts of excessive drinking.

During this time at the Academy he met one of the most famous composers in Russia, Borodin, who over a period of a few months introduced him to some of the other celebrated musicians of the day including Cui, Balakirev and Dargomizhky. Keeping such illustrious musical company obviously played an important part in inspiring Mussorgsky to write himself. His early efforts were not particularly good and his first two piano sonatas and a symphony have either been lost or were abandoned almost immediately. After a couple of years Mussorgsky realized that a life in the army was definitely not for him and he became profoundly interested in the arts – mainly music and literature.

He became increasingly interested in composition but found it difficult to deal with the problems of real life. He developed a bizarre sense of humour largely based on self-mockery and eventually only found solace in alcohol. The situation worsened when Tsar Alexander I liberated the serfs and the Mussorgsky family became impoverished. Modeste Mussorgsky had to take a job as a government clerk and the depression this caused him led to his first serious collapse at the hands of alcoholism. He was living in a commune with five other artistic young men but had to leave because of his ill health. He later moved in with his brother, who was tremendously supportive and encouraged his composing career.

Mussorgsky wrote some wonderful songs during this period and completed his opera based on the Pushkin play *Boris Godunov*. The first drafts of the opera were not very well received and he reworked it so that it is now a much respected full-length opera that is performed frequently around the world. Mussorgsky had also struck up a friendship with another composer, Rimsky-Korsakov, with whom he later shared a flat and who also made some revisions of *Boris Godunov*, helping it achieve the popularity it deserves.

Mussorgsky's career from then on was a mixture of ups and downs: the ups being good short bursts of creative work and the downs dreadful binges of drinking, losing jobs and being unable to complete his work through the effects of drink. He died following an epileptic fit and a few bouts of raging madness in the military hospital in St Petersburg on 28 March 1881, aged only forty-two.

Much of his music is worth exploring and in addition to the famous *Pictures at an Exhibition* (based on the drawings of a friend of his) and the *Night on a Bare Mountain*, Mussorgsky wrote some excellent songs which now rank alongside those of Schubert, Schumann and Wolf. Many people found his style of orchestration rather austere and a number of composers have since re-orchestrated his works with varying degrees of success. His close friend Rimsky-Korsakov, of course, revamped the opera *Boris Godunov* and the famous *Night on a Bare Mountain*, while Ravel splendidly orchestrated *Pictures at an Exhibition*. One other very different version of this piece is that by the seventies pop group Emerson, Lake and Palmer, who made the music accessible to a much wider audience than before. I prefer Mussorgsky's original version for piano, but other very striking versions are also to be found in the arrangements for brass group and wind orchestra as recorded by the Philip Jones Brass Ensemble and the New London Wind Orchestra respectively.

Recommended Listening

Pictures at an Exhibition (I/O – Ravel)
Boris Godunov (Op)
Songs and Dances of Death (V)
Night on a Bare Mountain (O)
The Nursery (V)

Further Listening

The Marriage (Op)
Khovanshchina (O)
Au village (I)
Impromptu Passionne (I)
Meditation (I)

Sergei Prokofiev (1891–1953)

One of the most popular and attractive of the Soviet composers, Prokofiev has a unique voice that finds a place at the very top of most people's lists of favourite twentieth-century composers. His music is witty, dramatic, poignant, brittle and ironic in flavour, yet always accessible and presented in a style that everyone can appreciate and enjoy. Interestingly enough, while Prokofiev's style is essentially twentieth-century and Russian in character, children of all nationalities find his music particularly captivating, with the *Troika* from the suite *Lieutenant Kije* and his narrated musical *Peter and the Wolf* being two enduring favourites.

Prokofiev was born into a very rich family in the

Ukraine. His father was an immensely successful businessman and his mother an accomplished amateur musician. He went to the conservatoire in St Petersburg at the age of thirteen, having amazed everyone with his prodigious talent – he wrote his first short piano pieces at the age of five and his first opera at the age of nine. He was immediately placed in the capable hands of Rimsky-Korsakov, who taught him until the outbreak of war in 1914.

Prokofiev's first piano concerto and sonata remain in the repertoire of many concert pianists today and these are essentially student works but already showed an extraordinary personality and individuality in their construction. The year 1917 saw the creation of his *Classical Symphony*, a work that cleverly combines a fusion of classical rhythms and melodic ideas with Prokofiev's uniquely twentieth-century Russian idiom.

Prokofiev lived in the United States for fifteen years from 1918 and his work received mixed reactions during that time. He was incredibly prolific and from this period came the opera *The Love for Three Oranges*, the *Piano Concertos Nos. 3, 4 and 5*, the *Symphonies Nos. 4 and 5*, and the ballet *The Prodigal Son*. Prokofiev found greater favour with European audiences and this period seems to have been a marvellous time of development that led on to another highly productive fifteen years, resident again in Russia.

The Russian authorities were strict about the development of music, literature and art at this time and Prokofiev was actually called up before the Central Committee in 1948 on charges of 'formalistic deviations' and 'democratic musical tendencies' – despite having scored the classic *Romeo and Juliet* ballet music, *Cinderella, Peter and the Wolf* and the *Violin Concerto No. 2*. In order to avoid huge confrontations and problems he wrote a letter admitting the charges and promised to rethink his work. The pieces that followed do not have the original spark of ingenuity and are positively bland in character compared to his earlier compositions, but they won him the Stalin Prize in

1951 and were works that the authorities approved of, even if Prokofiev was effectively writing with handcuffs on.

He died just two years later on 7 March 1953.

Recommended Listening

Romeo and Juliet (O)
Lieutenant Kije (O)
Piano Concerto No. 3 (O)
Classical Symphony (O)
Peter and the Wolf (O)

Further Listening

Piano Concerto No. 1 (O)
The Love for Three Oranges (Op)
Piano Sonata No. 6 (I)
The Prodigal Son (O)
Cinderella (O)

Igor Stravinsky (1882–1971)

Another outstanding musician from the twentieth century, Stravinsky has been one of the most innovative composers to have emerged in the last hundred years. He was born into a very musical family, his father being a highly successful bass-baritone in the Imperial Opera Company. Although encouraged in music as a boy and showing considerable talent, his parents refused to allow him to pursue a musical career and forced him to study criminal law and legal philosophy at the University of St Petersburg.

It did not take long, however, for Igor Stravinsky to make his own mind up and decide that he was going to be a composer. He organized private lessons in composition with Rimsky-Korsakov, who had also been Prokofiev's tutor and when his father died a few years later young Igor went all out to make his mark as a major figure in the world of music. His early orchestral work *Fireworks* was heard by Diaghilev, who was planning a series of Russian operas and ballets to be staged in Paris in 1909. Diaghilev was so impressed by Stravinsky's work that he commissioned him to write *The Firebird*, a ballet based on a Russian fairy-tale. This association with Diaghilev and the Russian Ballet Company continued when Stravinsky wrote *Petrushka* the following year and the controversial *Rite of Spring* in 1913.

The first performance of the *Rite of Spring* caused a riot. The audience were so shocked by the nature of the music and its subject – ritual sacrifice in primeval times – that they ended up shouting and screaming to the point that the dancers could no longer hear the music playing. It's an extraordinary piece of writing for the orchestra that has a profound effect on audiences in the concert hall to this day and there are sections from within this two-part work that have been the source of inspiration for numerous composers since, from both the classical field and the world of music for movies.

Because of the Russian Revolution in 1917, Stravinsky decided to remain in exile and not return to his homeland. The first work that he wrote thereafter was the marvellous music-theatre piece *The Soldier's Tale*, scored for a chamber ensemble and including parts for a dancer and narrators. Stravinsky made a resolution to include no references to his native land in this music and it was not until Diaghilev made contact again that Stravinsky had any connection with Russian subjects. He composed the music for another ballet entitled *Pulcinella* and this, again, avoided Russian stylistic references, being conceived as a neo-classical piece of music from Western European traditions.

Later that year, in 1920, the family moved from Switzerland to France and Stravinsky developed a side-line career both as a pianist and as a conductor. The next twenty years were very busy for him, writing and touring. Sadly, in 1938, his daughter died of consumption, while his wife and his mother lasted only one more year, both suffering from the same complaint.

The following year Stravinsky decided to leave France in search of a new life. He went to the United States and took up a post at Harvard University where he gave a set of six lectures on the Poetics of Music. He was very happy in America and in 1940 was joined by Vera de Bosset, a lady with whom he'd fallen in love some eighteen years earlier. They married and lived in Hollywood, where Stravinsky was inspired to write two of his finest works, the *Symphony in C* and the *Symphony in Three Movements*.

A few years later, in 1948, having signed a new publishing agreement with Boosey & Hawkes, Stravinsky was commissioned to write an opera, *The Rake's Progress*. This took three years to complete and was first performed in Venice in 1951 to great critical acclaim. His music from this period then took a turn away from the style that everyone had come to expect from him. He had been introduced to the works of the writers from the Second Viennese School and, having an interest in Webern's music in particular, started writing music using his own version of serialistic techniques (see the Second Viennese School).

In his last years Stravinsky was a much admired conductor and appeared with many of the leading international symphony orchestras. He also made recordings of many of his works which are still available and are well worth exploring. A bout of ill health followed and Stravinsky died in New York in 1971 aged eighty-nine and was buried in Venice.

Recommended Listening

The Rite of Spring (O)
The Firebird Suite (O)
Petrushka (O)
Pulcinella (O)
The Soldier's Tale (V/Ch)

Further Listening

The Nightingale (Op)
The Rake's Progress (Op)
Symphony in Three Movements (O)
Symphony of Psalms (O)
Violin Concerto in D (O)

Nicolai Rimsky-Korsakov (1844–1908)

Often very much underrated, Rimsky-Korsakov not only wrote many very fine and now popular works but also played an extremely important role in the whole development and history of Russian music. Many of the great Russian composers were taught by him and his extraordinary talent for orchestration was remarkable.

He came from a musical family and like most children of the day started to learn the piano at quite an early age when it was discovered that he possessed the rare gift of having perfect pitch. No-one really took much notice of any talent that he displayed and he was sent off to naval college in St Petersburg where he mixed with a number of people who were interested in music. His enthusiasm and enjoyment of music grew to the point when he moved into a circle of illustrious composers and began writing seriously himself. The other members of this clique were Cui, Borodin, Balakirev and Mussorgsky and they became known as 'The Five'.

Rimsky became a close friend of Mussorgsky and the two encouraged each other bouncing ideas around to their mutual benefit. Rimsky wrote nothing of any great stature during these early years and was regarded by many merely as a talented amateur, but he was gaining knowledge and developing his compositional technique all the while. In 1871 his talent was recognized and he was made a professor at the St Petersburg Conservatoire (although he later admitted that he was only a few pages ahead of his students when it came to harmony and counterpoint).

In 1873 he was given quite a prestigious job in the Navy as the Inspector of Military Bands.

Rimsky shared a flat with Mussorgsky and, as Mussorgsky was a chronic alcoholic, life was not easy. When eventually his flatmate died in 1881, Rimsky carried on with the task of orchestrating Mussorgsky's opera *Boris Godunov* and this is quite often the version that is performed today. The years rolled by and Rimsky wrote three works in 1888 that have now become the most popular of his output: *Capriccio Espagnol, Scheherazade* and the *Russian Easter Festival Overture*. He carried on writing operas and he was eventually regarded as the leading creative force in Russia at the time.

Nowadays, however, apart from the orchestral pieces already mentioned, most people know Rimsky-Korsakov for his amusing little piece *The Flight of the Bumblebee*, which has since been transcribed for almost every instrument imaginable as a showpiece of extraordinary virtuosity. Rimsky wrote an enormous amount of music, but we rarely get to hear very much of it owing to the preoccupation with the two or three favourites that sit alongside the works of Mussorgsky, Tchaikovsky, Prokofiev, Stravinsky and Rachmaninov. This is a shame, and I can confidently recommend the works in the lists that follow.

Recommended Listening

Capriccio Espagnol (O)
Russian Easter Festival Overture (O)
Scheherazade (O)
The Golden Cockerel (O)
The Flight of the Bumblebee (I)

May Night (Op)
Legend of the Invisible City of Kitezh (Op/O)
Tsar Sultan (Op/O)
Symphony No. 3 Op. 32 (O)
Skazka Op. 29 (O)

Dmitri Shostakovich (1906–75)

Renowned as one of the finest twentieth-century composers, Shostakovich has carved a definite niche as one of the finest symphonic writers since Tchaikovsky and Mahler. He has been described as a 'twentieth-century Beethoven' owing to the exceptional output of symphonies and chamber music that he managed in the face of quite severe adversity.

Shostakovich was born into a musical family who quickly recognized his prodigious talent. He studied at the St Petersburg Conservatoire and became an outstanding pianist. He faced the dilemma of whether to concentrate on being a pianist or a composer and elected for the latter, but once remarked: 'If the truth be told, I should have been both.'

A complex character, Shostakovich was fiercely critical of his own work and set himself inordinately high standards. He destroyed many of his earliest works but quickly found fame with the *Symphony No. 1*, performed in Leningrad in May 1926. However, in pursuit of fulfilling his own creative muse he soon faced opposition to many of his works. Audiences and critics alike found the music offensive, bourgeois, sensationalistic and incompatible with established Russian cultural traditions. This naturally upset Shostakovich but he reacted by continuing to write music that in the course of time has become standard repertoire for orchestras and performers throughout the world.

In 1936, following the harsh criticism of his 1934 opera

Lady Macbeth and a catastrophic rehearsal period of his subsequently withdrawn *Symphony No. 4* (only later to be performed in 1961!), he acknowledged the reaction and replied: 'I think art should be addressed to the people. They must be able to love and understand it; that is altogether essential. I try to use clear language – sometimes I succeed, sometimes not.' Whatever the reaction, Shostakovich did make a conscious effort to change his style and make his music more accessible even to the point of inscribing at the top of his *Symphony No. 5*: 'A Soviet artist's practical creative response to just criticism.' This is a truly marvellous work and has a slow movement of a beauty and intensity that have rarely been equalled by any composer in this century.

Shostakovich also had a talent for writing music for film and for theatre productions. His music for the ballet *The Bolt* shows another side to his creative genius as does the later *Age of Gold*, depicting the story of a Russian football team's visit to Western Europe. The music for the film *Hamlet*, written in 1963, is also a great example of his work in this style.

Shostakovich did not serve in the war: His eyesight was poor and he was refused entry into the Army on health grounds. He settled in Moscow with his family and took up a job at the Moscow Conservatoire. The postwar years saw Shostakovich come in for another bout of criticism for his failure to write music that provided inspiration for the Russian people. The authorities claimed his music was 'too difficult and not in line with the ideals of social realism'. He again weathered the storm, responding this time by writing some very patriotic works including his oratorio *The Song of the Forests* and the cantata *The Sun Shines Over Our Land*.

However, all the while he wrote music for his own satisfaction and to fulfil his own personal creative aspirations; hence the vast catalogue of piano music, string quartets and the later symphonies. The string quartets require special mention. These are intensely personal works, almost autobiographical in nature and listening to them can leave the listener both physically and emotionally drained.

Shostakovich was mad about sport and was a frequent visitor to football matches in particular, often much happier to travel hundreds of miles to an away game than to travel to give a concert. His health began to fail in the mid-sixties, but he kept writing throughout all the troubles in his life; and this period of ill health did not cause any lack of creativity. In fact he wrote a number of exceptional works including the last four string quartets and the *Symphonies Nos. 14 and 15*. Shostakovich came to London to hear the first British performance of his *Symphony No. 15* (containing little quotes from the famous *William Tell Overture* and Wagner's *Ring*!) conducted by his son Maxim. This was at the Royal Festival Hall and it was quite clear that he was feeling frail. He died a few years later in a Moscow hospital on 9 August 1975.

Audiences are quite often frightened by the sight of Shostakovich's works on a concert programme. For some reason aside from the reputation attached to his compositions by the Soviet authorities, the actual name Shostakovich sounds rather imposing. Do not be put off! Try the two *Piano Concertos* for a gentle and pleasant introduction to his music and work on through to the *Symphony No. 5* and perhaps the *String Quartet No. 3*. If you enjoy these works, there is no reason why you shouldn't enjoy the rest of the catalogue. He was a masterful composer who has a very relevant voice in the world of twentieth-century music.

RECOMMENDED LISTENING

Piano Concerto No. 1 (O)
Symphony No. 5 (O)
The Age of Gold (O)
String Quartet No. 3 (Ch)
Cello Concertos Nos. 1 and 2 (O)

FURTHER LISTENING

Hamlet (O)
Symphony No. 10 (O)
String Quartet No. 15 (Ch)
Katerina Izmaylova (Op)
Twenty-four Preludes and Fugues (I)
Piano Quintet in G minor Op. 57 (Ch)

Jean Sibelius (1865–1957)

Sibelius holds a very special place in the history of Scandinavian music, not only because he is really the one composer of note to have come from Finland but also because he had a very serious interest in Finnish mythology and culture which he's portrayed in his music.

The son of a doctor, Sibelius was christened Johan Julius Christian but adopted the name Jean having found a set of visiting-cards belonging to his seafaring uncle, who had gallicized the name. Jean's father died of cholera when the boy was just two years old and so young Sibelius was brought up by his grandmother who placed him at a Finnish-speaking school. This was quite unusual at the time, as much of Finland was Swedish-speaking owing to being governed by a Swedish-speaking minority.

He started to compose at the age of ten. A piece for violin and cello entitled *Water Drops* was followed by a number of other smaller chamber works that have a youthful naïveté about them and are rarely heard these days. Sibelius was very keen on playing the violin, always having a passionate yearning to be a professional violinist and he apparently even went to the lengths of auditioning for the strings of the Vienna Philharmonic Orchestra.

Like many composers, his early studies at university were in a totally unrelated subject – in his case, law – but he soon gave this up in favour of a course in music. It was at Helsinki University that he struck up a friendship with the Italian composer Feruccio Busoni, who later gave

Sibelius an introduction to Brahms. After a couple of years Sibelius wrote the *Kullervo Symphony*, which established him as a first-rate composer and this was followed by a selection of wonderful works including *Finlandia*, the *Valse triste* and a string of symphonies all of which hold firm places in the repertoire of most international symphony orchestras.

Sibelius was a colourful character who liked nothing better than to drink vast quantities of alcohol and smoke fat cigars. Both activities were severely curtailed when he developed a serious illness in 1908 and had to undergo a series of operations for what was diagnosed as cancer of the throat. These operations were apparently successful as he lived for almost another fifty years, although his composing really stopped around 1926 when he wrote the incidental music for a performance of Shakespeare's *The Tempest*.

Sibelius was a keen traveller and made regular visits to England, France, Germany and Italy and he was also in demand as a conductor, which it seemed was compensation for his not becoming a concert violinist. He was honoured with numerous awards, among which were the Chair of Composition at the Imperial Academy (1912) and an honorary doctorate at Yale University, following his enormous successes in America. His music has a beautiful blend of romanticism and drama, always with the flavour of his native country, Finland, flowing through. The earlier works like *Finlandia* and the first few symphonies are wonderful easy listening and the later *Symphonies Nos. 5 and 7* are also of particular interest.

Recommended Listening

Finlandia (O)
Violin Concerto (O)
En Saga (O)
Symphony No. 2 (O)
Valse triste (I)

Tapiola (O)
The Swan of Tuonela (O)
The Tempest (O)
Pelléas et Mélisande (O)
Symphony No. 5 (O)

Edvard Grieg (1843–1907)

A few years ago, Nescafé ran a television commercial that provoked an enormous number of enquiries about the nature of the soundtrack. It was *'Morning'* taken from Grieg's *Peer Gynt Suite*. Grieg, I would say, is Norway's greatest composer, while less charitable musicologists might say 'Norway's *only* great composer'. Whatever their views, Grieg holds a highly regarded place in classical circles as the composer of one of the most popular piano concertos of all time. He has also given us an insight into the folk culture and character of his native land through his music in the same way that Dvořák, Smetana, Copland, Sibelius and Elgar have done for their respective countries.

Originally of Scottish descent on his father's side, it seems that Grieg may have received his extraordinary musical abilities from his mother, who was an accomplished pianist. She gave her son piano lessons from the age of six and Grieg showed such excellent promise that he was sent off to study at the illustrious Leipzig Conservatoire where he was heavily influenced by Robert Schumann. He found his time in Leipzig totally absorbing and made a point of attending concerts and utilizing his time as a student to the very best advantage.

In 1863 he moved to Copenhagen, the cultural capital of Scandinavia and it was here that Grieg really became interested in folk culture. He spent the next few years travelling between each of the three countries (Denmark, Finland and Norway) and in 1865 composed the *Peer Gynt*

Suite for Henrik Ibsen's drama. This was one of his earliest-known compositions and it was followed by his first *Sonata for Violin* and the *Piano Sonata*.

Grieg eventually settled in Norway in 1866 and founded the Norwegian Academy of Music – a bold step for a man of just twenty-three years of age. He felt passionately about promoting the works of all Norwegian composers and frequently arranged concert tours to widen the appreciation of this music. Just two years later, Grieg wrote his celebrated *Piano Concerto in A minor*, the opening of which most people will recognize when they hear it. It really is a marvellous work and is surprisingly the only composition of considerable length and development that Grieg wrote. He was the master of writing short folk-style pieces and never felt driven to write in the extended forms that many of his contemporaries were employing. He did have a go at writing a second piano concerto but soon gave up, realizing that works on this scale were not his strong point.

He appears to have been an endearing man, holding his nationalistic traditions dear and he took an active stance in promoting new and young talent, demonstrated by founding the Norwegian Academy of Music. He was also a marvellous after-dinner speaker with a wit that was much appreciated by all who heard him. Grieg was for most of his life a lonely figure despite marrying his cousin Nina Hagerup in 1866.

Recommended Listening

Peer Gynt Suite (O)
Piano Concerto in A minor Op. 16 (O)
Holberg Suite Op. 40 (O)
Sonata for Cello and Piano (Ch)
Sigurd Jorsalfar Op. 22 (O)

Four Norwegian Dances Op. 35 (O)
Sonata for Violin and Piano No. 3 (Ch)
String Quartet in G (Ch)
Symphonic Dances (O)
Lyric Pieces (I)

George Gershwin (1898–1937)

George Gershwin was the second son of Moishe Gershovitza, a Russian Jew who had settled in the United States in about 1890 and promptly changed his name to Morris Gershvin. Moishe was an intensely ambitious man who was also striving to better himself and his family's situation. Rumour has it that they moved house some twenty-eight times in less than twenty years and that during that time Moishe had as many jobs! George was christened Jacob, while his elder brother Ira was originally christened Israel (later to be known as Izzy).

Young George showed his first real interest in music when he heard an automatic piano playing Rubinstein's *Melody in F* and from then on developed an uncontrollable fascination with the subject. The family acquired a piano that was originally intended for Ira's use, but George was able immediately to sit down and work out some of the popular tunes and ragtime music that he was particularly keen on at the time. He had lessons with a local lady and then went on to study with Charles Hambitzer, who had a profound effect on his development. It was already clear that George was destined for great things – either as a concert pianist or as a composer – and it was no secret that he was happiest playing pop and jazz music.

He left school at the age of fifteen and immediately got a job as a staff pianist at the Tin Pan Alley firm of Jerome H. Remick & Co. He was only required to accompany song-pluggers and was soon dissatisfied with his lot, particularly as his own first attempts at song-writing were turned down by the company.

Undeterred, George kept writing and scored his first publishing hit with a song called *'When You Want 'Em You Can't Get 'Em: When You've Got 'Em You Don't Want 'Em'*, which was published in 1916. He went on to write a quick succession of hits including songs that were incorporated into other people's shows – a famous example being the song *'Swanee'* used in Al Jolson's show *Sinbad*.

Gershwin really hit the headlines with his ever popular *Rhapsody in Blue*, a jazzy concerto for piano with orchestra (or band), first performed in 1924. There followed a series of commissions and the *Piano Concerto in F*, which was written and performed just one year later, is now a standard piece on the concert platform. George's brother Ira was a very talented lyric-writer and the two collaborated on songs and shows throughout George's tragically short career. *Lady Be Good*, starring the Astaires, was one of their first hits.

One of George's best-known works is the folk-opera *Porgy and Bess*, written in 1935 and this contains the ever popular song *'Summertime'*, performed all over the world in every style imaginable. His rhapsodic symphonic work *An American in Paris* is also a big favourite with audiences, while serious concert pianists often include his remarkable *Three Preludes* in their programmes.

RECOMMENDED LISTENING

Rhapsody in Blue (O)
An American in Paris (O)
Porgy and Bess (Op)
Piano Concerto in F (O)
Three Preludes for Piano (I)

Cuban Overture (O)
Second Rhapsody (O)
Variations on 'I Got Rhythm' (I)
'Someone to Watch Over Me' (V)
'Strike Up the Band' (V)

Aaron Copland (1900–91)

Aaron Copland's parents were Russian Jews who emigrated to the United States. Their name was originally Kaplan; but this was misspelt by the immigration authorities, so Copland it was.

Copland did not show any great aptitude for music until about the age of eleven, when his sister was having piano lessons. He was quite inspired by the music she was playing and decided that he would like to have lessons himself. Fascinated, too, by the whole art of creating music, he had lessons in harmony and composition with Rubin Goldmark when he was about seventeen. Copland desperately wanted to pursue his interest in music and four years later made his way to Paris to study with Nadia Boulanger (a celebrated and much revered musicologist).

He returned to America some seven years later, having absorbed the modernist influences of Paris and Madame Boulanger. In 1925 his *Symphony for Organ and Orchestra* was performed and the conductor Damrosch turned to the audience and said: 'If a young man at twenty-three can write a symphony like that, in five years' time he'll be ready to commit murder!' This appears not to have bothered Copland too much at the time, but as the years passed he began to address this most serious of issues – the relationship between the composer and the audience. This is a matter that many of today's composers are guilty of neglecting, which is why public interest is not great for much of what has been produced in recent years.

Cast your mind back to the days of Bach and Handel

or Mozart and Haydn, when the public couldn't wait to hear the latest works of these composers and would make a point of being present at the first performances. Nowadays composers are lucky to see a sprinkling of academic admirers alongside the critics at the first performances of their works, with many people being confused and bewildered at the musical assaults they are subjected to. Copland became aware of this and astutely took it on board. He then began to write from the heart – romantic music with a distinctly American flavour to it. *El Salon Mexico* was followed by the ballet *Billy the Kid, An Outdoor Overture, Quiet City, Rodeo* and in 1945 the much-loved *Appalachian Spring* ballet music. Copland was honoured with the Pulitzer Prize and the award of the New York Music Critics for *Appalachian Spring* and this piece paved the way for Copland's longest work, the *Symphony No. 3*, which has been described as being 'all about America'. Copland's music sits perfectly alongside that of George Gershwin: Gershwin with his jazzy populist style and Copland with his amazing gift for writing music that captures the spirit of 'the American great outdoors'.

Recommended Listening

Appalachian Spring (O)
Billy the Kid (O)
Rodeo (O)
An Outdoor Overture (O)
El Salon Mexico (O)

Further Listening

Quiet City (O)
The Tender Land (Op)
Old American Songs (V/O)
Clarinet Concerto (O)
Dance Symphony 1929 (O)

Where to Go from Here in the Nationalistic Styles

Czechoslovakia:

Martinu

Scandinavia:

Berwald, Nielsen

Russia:

Glinka, Borodin, Balakirev, Cui, Scriabin, Glazunov

United States of America:

Ives, Bernstein, Carter

French Nationalists:

Poulenc, Milhaud, Satie

Spanish Nationalists:

De Falla, Granados, Albeniz

South America:

Villa Lobos

THE SECOND VIENNESE SCHOOL

This school of composers includes Arnold Schoenberg (1874–1951), Anton von Webern (1883–1945) and Alban Berg (1885–1935). Schoenberg was the founder of the school and introduced the concept of 'serialistic techniques' for composing music. This is sometimes referred to as the 'twelve tone' system: The twelve notes of a scale are arranged in a specific order to form a 'series' or a 'tone row' and this becomes the basic element of the composition. The series can then be developed by turning it upside down, back to front, transposed or upside down and back to front! The one golden rule is that the composer must not repeat any single note before first having used all the others in the series. If this sounds odd to you, don't worry – it certainly sounds odd to me, too!

The results using this system of composing are often extremely weird and the music can sound bland, totally tuneless and without form (very strange when such a significant formal treatment has been applied). I can, however, cite examples of pieces that have been written using this technique that are quite effective: Passages in Schoenberg's *Concerto for Violin* have moments of great beauty, but in the main, this style of music is to be approached with extreme caution.

Schoenberg started off life as a banker, which may explain his preoccupation with writing music using mathematical techniques. He hated the job and eventually turned to composing and teaching music full time. His finest works are listed below and while I've obviously given a cautionary word of warning for people interested in dabbling in this esoteric style of classical music, I can confidently recommend your listening to the pieces listed.

Anton von Webern and Alban Berg were pupils of Schoenberg. Berg's music is perhaps the most approachable of the three, being more romantic and accessible in style, whilst Webern wrote short, powerful and challenging pieces with very stark textures.

Berg wrote two operas that are regarded as significant contributions to the whole development of opera in the twentieth century – *Wozzeck* and *Lulu*. His *Violin Concerto* is an absolute masterpiece while his *Piano Sonata Op. 1* (written before he got tied up with these serialistic influences) is an out and out piece of romantic music following closely in the footsteps of Mahler and Brahms.

Webern, on the other hand, is altogether more challenging. He wrote very few works and those he did write are mostly very short; the *Five Pieces for Orchestra* are a case in point, being only 76 bars long. Some would say he was the first of the minimalists and it is interesting to have a listen to some of his music if the opportunity arises. Try the *Six Bagatelles for String Quartet* as a starting point and see how you feel about it all from there. If it's possible, make a point of listening out for the twelve-tone row and see if you can spot its reappearance in different guises. Webern was also a master of applying serialistic techniques to all the parameters in the music – the dynamics, the duration of sections and the octave-pitch of individual notes, for example, but this is perhaps best seen when studying the score.

Recommended Listening

SCHOENBERG:
Chamber Symphony Op. 9 (O)
Pierrot Lunaire (V/Ch)
Verklarte Nacht (Ch/O)
Pelléas und Mélisande (O)

ANTON VON WEBERN:
Six Bagatelles for String Quartet (Ch)
Five Pieces for Small Orchestra (O)
Songs Op. 17 (V)

ALBAN BERG:
Piano Sonata Op. 1 (I)
Violin Concerto (O)
Wozzeck (Op)
Lulu (Op)
Three Orchestral Pieces (O)

CHAPTER FOUR

A Brief Look at Opera

Opera is a subject too large to tackle fully within the confines of this book but in recent years a number of performers of operatic works have helped to make this side of classical music popular to a completely new audience. It seems appropriate, then, to include a short note on some of the most famous operatic composers with a selection of short pieces for you to explore both as examples of fine music and as an introduction to opera itself.

The 'Three Tenors' concert from Italy during the 1990 World Cup celebrations really triggered the whole thing off. Pavarotti's heartrending version of Puccini's *'Nessun dorma'* (from the opera *Turandot*) will stay firmly in our memory, not only as a wonderful piece of music but also as a reminder of a fantastic sporting event.

The Top Fifty Composers section of this book includes some great musicians for whom opera was just one of the things they did well. Mozart, for instance, composed some of the finest operas ever written, including *The Marriage of Figaro, Don Giovanni, The Magic Flute,* and *Così Fan Tutte*. Beethoven wrote one giant opera, *Fidelio*. Berlioz's

The Trojans, Richard Strauss' *Der Rosenkavalier* and Rossini's *The Barber of Seville* are all part of the standard repertoire of leading operatic companies. In this section, though, I want to introduce you to a few composers who made opera their main business.

Bizet's *Carmen* is one of the most famous and accessible of all operas and this would be an excellent one with which to make your first acquaintance. Alan 'Fluff' Freeman has long championed a short extract from the '*Toreador's Song*' in one of his 'classic' jingles – everyone knows this one when they hear it! Other than this particular opera (Bizet's most popular piece), I have chosen four composers whose works will also provide the best introduction to opera. They have been chosen not simply because they have all written great operas, but because there are many recordings available that present highlights from their most popular works. If you want to get a taste of what their music is all about, it will be easy for you to go and make your selections in a record shop. I must stress, though, that listening to the music is just part of the 'complete experience'. You really do need to see the opera to make the whole thing come alive.

Gioacchino Rossini (1792–1868)

Composer of many famous popular classics such as *William Tell* and *The Barber of Seville*, the story of Rossini's life is an extraordinary one. He wrote all his best music within twenty years and then at the age of thirty-seven almost stopped altogether and spent the last thirty years of his life in retirement! There are a number of theories as to why this happened, the most popular being that it was a combination of ill health (mental rather than physical), disappointment at the poor response to his opera *William Tell* and a serious love of relaxing and having a good time!

Rossini was very much the pop-music composer of his

day and people used to go around humming and whistling their favourite Rossini tunes.

Not to be missed are recordings of the overtures from his operas, including the famous *William Tell, The Thieving Magpie, The Barber of Seville, The Italian Girl in Algiers* and *Semiramide.*

Giacomo Puccini (1858–1924)

Mention Pavarotti or *'Nessun dorma'* and everyone will relate to that highly charged performance that has now made Puccini famous the world over. Pavarotti's version of *'Nessun dorma'* outsold all other records in the summer of 1990 and captured the hearts of millions who had never even heard an opera before. Puccini's music really does have something special about it and actually succeeded in creating a whole new audience almost overnight.

He wrote many more good tunes like that one from *Turandot* and out of his dozen or so operas the three most popular are: *La Bohème, Madam Butterfly* and *Tosca.* They are all brilliant and demonstrate Puccini's unique gift for writing memorable melodies and for capturing the audience's attention with pure dramatic intensity. Some would criticize him for being populist, in a way that Verdi and Wagner were not, but no-one can disagree that Puccini showed a clear understanding of what people want to hear and see at the opera.

Famous Puccini arias are in abundance and I can thoroughly recommend '*Your Tiny Hand Is Frozen*' and '*They Call Me Mimi*' from *La Bohème,* '*Love and Music*' and '*The Stars Are Shining Brightly*' from *Tosca,* and '*One Fine Day*' from *Madam Butterfly* – not forgetting '*Nessun dorma*' from the slightly lesser known *Turandot.*

Don't be afraid to listen to the whole of these operas. Within the CD or record sets you will usually find a translation of the libretto. It could open up a whole new world for you.

Giuseppe Verdi (1813–1901)

Aida is one of the most popular operas of all time and is the one that I would lead you to for an introduction to Verdi's work. It's magnificent and is just one of twenty-six that he composed, of which about fifteen or sixteen are still regularly performed in major opera houses around the world.

One of Verdi's other most popular pieces is his *Requiem*, and while this is not an opera it is very operatic in style with dramatic arias sung by the solo singers and off-stage trumpeters providing dramatic bursts. But it is for writing operas that Verdi has now become a household name and he, like Puccini, had the gift of writing memorable tunes.

When compared with Puccini, Verdi chose more serious stories and subject-matter on which to base his operas and among his most famous are *Nabucco, Aida, Rigoletto, La Traviata, Don Carlos, Il Trovatore, Macbeth, Otello* and *Falstaff*.

Richard Wagner (1813–83)

One of the most influential composers of all time, Wagner unquestionably changed the course of both opera and classical music in general. He developed the marvellous concept of what he described as 'total art work', which employed the mediums of music and drama to convey political, psychological, emotional and ethical issues within the framework of a work of art – his 'music dramas' as he preferred them to be called.

Wagner's works are on a grand scale, usually with a very large orchestra and a huge chorus. The music is normally continuous, unlike most other operas where there are individual arias and choruses, sometimes interspersed with dialogue. Seeing a Wagner opera is more akin to taking part in an epic movie and the intensity and dramatic impact of these works are totally absorbing.

He is most famous for his cycle of operas, *The Ring*,

four 'music dramas' based on the story of a power struggle between ancient gods, giants, dwarfs and humans. This is strong stuff and can be approached on two levels: Simply as a piece of extraordinary music drama, or as a study of the parallels Wagner was drawing between myth and reality, good and evil, primitive and contemporary society. It has to be left to the listener to judge for himself whether or not Wagner was making political statements within his work and, as you will discover, this has been the subject of much discussion among musicians, opera-goers and musicologists for the past hundred years.

A number of recordings exist of the preludes to his operas and these will give you an idea as to the flavour of the music. For a true picture of the vocal impact that Wagner's music can have, do explore any of the recordings that are available presenting highlights of some of the more popular sections of his works. Titles to look out for include: *Tannhäuser, Lohengrin, Tristan und Isolde, Die Meistersinger von Nürnberg, Parsifal* and *The Ring*.

CHAPTER FIVE

Where Next?

If you have had a chance to listen to the tape and you've also read the book thus far, you quite probably have a good idea of the styles of classical music that you like. There are two other routes that you can now take, having ascertained your immediate preferences and these are either to go back in time and see where it all came from or to come forward to the present day and explore what is being written right now.

Going back to pre-Baroque music is an interesting option. There are a number of really wonderful composers who were writing sacred music in the sixteenth and early seventeenth century. Italy is where it was mainly happening, with Monteverdi and Palestrina being the models for a whole host of other composers writing at the time. Andrea and Giovanni Gabrieli were also highly respected composers of church music, while Girolamo Frescobaldi followed on from where they left off and became known as one of the finest writers of instrumental works in the early part of the seventeenth century.

In England, composers like Thomas Tallis, Thomas Morley, John Dowland and Orlando Gibbons were highly thought of and I can thoroughly recommend you to explore works by any of these if you are interested in this earlier period of music.

One could also go back a stage or two further and listen to medieval music, which has experienced a definite rise in popularity over the last ten years. There are a number of specialist groups who perform only medieval music and it would be a good idea to sample a couple of compilation albums to ascertain where your preferences may lie within this genre.

So what about the music that is being written today? Those of you who have heard classical music that was written in the seventies and eighties will have your own opinions. If you haven't come across any of this material one solution is to listen to BBC Radio 3. It broadcasts programmes entitled 'Music in Our Time', among others, that are solely dedicated to presenting the music of today. Without wishing to make any sweeping generalizations (and here comes one straight away!), much of this music is cacophonous, discordant, unpleasant and difficult to understand. Many professional musicians also find it so. Don't automatically feel that just because you are essentially a lay person when it comes to music, it's through ignorance that you feel uncomfortable with a certain type of music. Not only is a lot of contemporary music difficult both to play and to listen to but it can be unrewarding as well. Therefore, extreme care should be taken when selecting what material you are going to try by way of an introduction.

My advice is to ease in gently with the music of some of the minimalist composers like Steve Reich, John Adams and Philip Glass. Minimalist music is music that uses small fragments of melody, rhythm and harmony and by repetition and variation creates something of a hypnotic effect on the listener. Reich's *Desert Song* is a great work, while John Adams's opera *Nixon in China* has a power and intensity that is extremely dramatic, while also being exciting and pleasurable to listen to.

There are a handful of celebrated composers who have

written what will quite probably become 'classics' in years to come and my own personal recommendations include Witold Lutoslawski (Polish), Luciano Berio (Italian), Hans Werner Henze (German), Harrison Birtwistle (English), Peter Maxwell Davies (English), Gyorgy Ligeti (Hungarian) who provided much of the music to the film *2001: A Space Odyssey*, and Olivier Messiaen (French) whose *Quartet for the End of Time*, written while he was a prisoner in the Second World War, is one of the most moving and emotional pieces that I know.

There are also a few young composers emerging in Britain who are ignoring the rather scholarly, mathematical, formal styles of classical music that have developed over the last thirty or forty years, in favour of a more direct means of expression utilizing the established traditions of melody, harmony and rhythm – and why not? These are the very elements of classical music that we've become accustomed to and it seems wholly appropriate to use these devices in a way that is relevant to today's expression through the medium of music. Dave Heath springs to mind as being someone who can successfully combine traditional classical notation with the sounds of today, invariably calling upon the performers to use techniques more akin to pop music – the effects of which are often extremely exciting. Judging by audience reactions over the last few years, we will no doubt be hearing a lot more from him. By way of an introduction to the music of Reich, Glass, Adams and Heath, I can thoroughly recommend a recording on the Virgin Classics label by the LCO entitled *LCO 8* that encompasses works by all four composers and this would be an effective way of sampling all their works in one go.

In America, composers like John Cage and Elliot Carter have also had a big impact on the development of classical music in the twentieth century. John Cage is famous for his piece *4' 33"*, in which the performer makes no sound during that time; the 'music' is literally just the sound of the ambient noise in the concert hall! His other works are equally bizarre and include *Imaginary Landscape No. 4* for twelve radios and *HPSCHD* which is for one to seven harpsichords and one to fifty-one tape machines. Elliot Carter's music is completely different. Following more in the traditions of Copland, his music is more overtly American in nature, is difficult, noisy and often abrasive to the ear. However, I would say that to make an effort to get to know some of his music could be a very rewarding experience. Try his suite to the ballet *The Minotaur* or the *Variations for Orchestra.* I must reiterate my warning: This is not music for the faint-hearted!

Don't be frightened – be adventurous. Try to hear the music live in the concert hall; the combination of the atmosphere and seeing the performers in action will help you feel a part of the whole experience and should assist your enjoyment of the music as well. There is music out there that is good and which will communicate something to you. There are, as I say, a number of fine composers who are genuinely attempting to express themselves in a way that audiences today can understand and making the effort to get to grips with their music will often be rewarding and enjoyable. Equally, don't be afraid to trust your intuition; if you think what you are listening to sounds more like a couple of mechanics working in a breaker's yard you're more than likely going to be right and in good company in thinking so.

I cannot conclude this section without referring to a work by one of Britain's most popular composers of musicals who has ventured into the realms of classical music: Andrew Lloyd Webber's *Requiem.* He wrote this piece a couple of years ago and utilized the standard format of a normal classical requiem – a large orchestra, vocal soloists and a chorus. The performances and recordings made include such celebrated artists as José Carreras, Sarah Brightman, Paul Miles-Kington and the renowned conductor Lorin Maazel.

It's a work that is immediately accessible and has moments of beauty, although many might criticize it for being somewhat derivative. However, it achieved mass popularity – many thousands of records sold and a number of very well-attended live concert performances – both rarely achieved by most other composers in the classical music scene today.

Wherever your taste and preferences lie, whether it be in the mainstream classics, early music composers or the music of today – Happy hunting!

CHAPTER SIX

Music Made Famous in Films and Commercials

The music used on the soundtrack of a film or a television commercial has a vital role to play in creating just the right atmosphere. It's no wonder, then, that film-makers and producers have 'sourced' some of the most memorable soundtracks from the classical repertoire and I have listed here some of the most famous, in the hope that it may provide the answers to those burning questions 'What exactly was that music in the film *Fatal Attraction*?' and 'Where can I find the music to the Hovis commercial?'

MUSIC FROM THE MOVIES

10	Ravel: *Bolero*
2001: A SPACE ODYSSEY	Richard Strauss: *Also Sprach Zarathustra Op. 30*

A CLOCKWORK ORANGE	Elgar: *Pomp and Circumstance March No. 1* Rossini: *William Tell Overture* Beethoven: *Symphony No. 9 ('Choral')*
ALIEN	Hanson: *Symphony No. 2 ('Romantic')*
APOCALYPSE NOW	Wagner: *Die Walküre*
A ROOM WITH A VIEW	Puccini: *Gianni Schicchi* ('*O mio babbino caro*')
BRIEF ENCOUNTER	Rachmaninov: *Piano Concerto No. 2*
DEATH IN VENICE	Mahler: *Symphony No. 5 in C sharp minor*
DIE HARD 2	Sibelius: *Finlandia Op. 26*
DIVA	Catalina: *La Wally*
DRIVING MISS DAISY	Dvořák: '*Song to the Moon*'
ELVIRA MADIGAN	Mozart: *Piano Concerto No. 21 in C major*
EXCALIBUR	Carl Orff: *Carmina Burana*
FATAL ATTRACTION	Puccini: *Madam Butterfly*
GALLIPOLI	Albinoni: *Adagio in G major*
HANNAH AND HER SISTERS	Bach: *Harpsichord Concerto No. 5; Concerto for Two Violins, BWV 1053*

HEAT AND DUST	Johann Strauss II: '*Tales from the Vienna Woods*'
KRAMER VS KRAMER	Vivaldi: *Mandolin Concerto*
MY LEFT FOOT	Mozart: *Così fan tutte*
ORDINARY PEOPLE	Pachelbel: *Canon*
OUT OF AFRICA	Mozart: *Clarinet Concerto in A, K. 622*
PLATOON	Samuel Barber: *Adagio for Strings Op. 11*
PRIZZI'S HONOUR	Donizetti: *L'Elisir d'amore*
SLEEPING WITH THE ENEMY	Berlioz: *Symphonie fantastique*
THE ELEPHANT MAN	Samuel Barber: *Adagio for Strings Op. 11*
THE KILLING FIELDS	Puccini: *Turandot* ('*Nessun dorma*')
THE WITCHES OF EASTWICK	Puccini: *Turandot* ('*Nessun dorma*')
WHO FRAMED ROGER RABBIT?	Liszt: *Hungarian Rhapsody No. 2*

MUSIC IN COMMERCIALS

ALLIED DUNBAR INSURANCE	Elgar: *Chanson de matin*

AUDI	Schubert: *Symphony No. 8* (*'Unfinished'*)
BATCHELOR SOUPS	Mozart: *Eine Kleine Nachtmusik*
BACO FOIL	Tchaikovsky: *1812 Overture*
BAILEYS IRISH CREAM	Offenbach: *Tales of Hoffman*
BARCLAYS BANK	Tchaikovsky: *Symphony No. 6*
BLACK & DECKER PAINT-STRIPPER	Rimsky-Korsakov: *Flight of the Bumblebee*
BLACK & DECKER	Tchaikovsky: *Francesca da Rimini*
BLUE BAND	Beethoven: *Symphony No. 6*
BOLD WASHING POWDER	Catalina: *La Wally*
BOSCH	Paganini: *Mouvement perpetuel*
BOURNEVILLE	Chopin: *'Tristesse' Étude in E major*
BRAUN	Vivaldi: *Four Seasons* (*'Winter'*)
BRITISH AIRWAYS	Verdi: *Nabucco* (*'Chorus of the Hebrew Slaves'*) Delibes: *Lakmé*
BRITISH STEEL	Elgar: *Symphony No. 1*

BRITISH TELECOM	Ravel: *Daphnis and Chloé* (*'Daybreak'*) Schumann: *Kinderszenen*
BUXTON SPRING WATER	Elgar: *Cello Concerto*
CADBURY'S FRUIT AND NUT	Tchaikovsky: *Nutcracker Suite* (*'Dance of the Sugar Plum Fairy'*)
CAMPBELLS SOUPS	Puccini: *Madam Butterfly*
CARLSBERG	Schubert: *Symphony No. 8* (*'Unfinished'*)
CASTROL OIL	Mahler: *Symphony No. 7*
CINZANO	Liszt: *Liebesträume*
CITROËN BX	Vivaldi: *Four Seasons* (*'Winter'*)
CLARKES SHOES	Prokofiev: *Peter and the Wolf*
COALITE	Mendelssohn: *Symphony No. 4* (*'Italian'*)
DREAM TOPPING	Tchaikovsky: *Nutcracker Suite* (*'Dance of the Sugar Plum Fairy'*)
ELECTRICITY COUNCIL	Beethoven: *Symphony No. 3* (*'Eroica'*)
THE EUROPEAN	Beethoven: *Symphony No. 9* (*'Ode to Joy'*)
FIAT MIRAFIORI	Verdi: *Rigoletto* (*'La donna e mobile'*)

Fiat Strada	Rossini: *Barber of Seville*
Fiesta Kitchen Towels	Dukas: *Sorcerer's Apprentice*
Findus Dinner	Puccini: *Gianni Schicchi* ('*O mio babbino caro*')
Gayles Honey	Rimsky-Korsakov: *Flight of the Bumblebee*
Gillette	Catalani: *La Wally*
Gold Seal Batteries	Bizet: *Carmen* ('*Toreador's Song*')
The Guardian	Haydn: *Symphony No. 10*
Guinness	Tchaikovsky: *Romeo and Juliet*
Hamlet Cigars	Bach: *Air on the G String*
Heineken	Albinoni: *Adagio* Rossini: *William Tell Overture*
Hovis	Dvořák: *Symphony No. 9* ('*New World*')
IBM Computers	Beethoven: '*Für Elise*'
Kleenex	Mascagni: *Cavalleria Rusticana*
Legal & General	Haydn: *Symphony No. 94* ('*Surprise*')

LLOYDS BANK	Bach: *Cantata No. 140 (4th movement)*
LUFTHANSA	Mozart: *Symphony No. 40 in G minor*
LYONS COFFEE	Johann Strauss II: '*Blue Danube*'
MAXELL TAPES	Mussorgsky: *Night on a Bare Mountain*
MR SHEEN	Rossini: *William Tell Overture*
NESCAFÉ	Grieg: *Peer Gynt Suite* ('*Morning*')
OLD SPICE AFTERSHAVE	Orff: *Carmina Burana*
P & O SEA PRINCESS	Smetana: *Ma Vlast* ('*Vltava*')
PEAUDOUCE	Ponchielli: *La Giaconda* ('*Dance of the Hours*')
PEUGOT 605	Smetana: *Ma Vlast*
PEDIGREE CHUM	Dvořák: *Symphony No. 9* ('*New World*')
PIRELLI	Puccini: *Turandot* ('*Nessun dorma*')
POMAGNE	Delibes: *Sylvia* (*Pizzicato*)
PRETTY POLLY	Puccini: *Tosca* ('*Mario*')
PURE NEW WOOL (1970–80)	Beethoven: *Symphony No. 6* ('*Pastoral*')

PURE NEW WOOL (1990)	Pachelbel: *Canon*
RIDGEWAYS TEA	Debussy: *Claire de lune*
ROWENTA COFFEE-MAKER	Vivaldi: *Four Seasons* (*'Spring'*)
ROYAL BANK OF SCOTLAND	Mussorgsky: *Pictures at an Exhibition* Britten: *Simple Symphony* (*'Playful Pizzicato'*)
RYVITA	Ravel: *Bolero*
ST BRUNO	Elgar: *'Enigma' Variations* (*'Nimrod'*)
SCHWEPPES MALVERN WATER	Elgar: *Symphony No. 1*
STREPSILS	Satie: *Gymnopédie No. 3*
SWAN LIGHT LAGER	Tchaikovsky: *Swan Lake* (*'Dance of the Swans'*)
TODAY	Verdi: *Requiem* (*'Dies Irae'*)
TWEED PERFUME	Beethoven: *Symphony No. 6* (*'Pastoral'*)
VAUXHALL ASTRA	Elgar: *Pomp and Circumstance March No. 4*
VAUXHALL BELMONT	Bizet: *Pearl Fishers* (*Duet*)
VAUXHALL CARLTON	Mozart: *Horn Concerto No. 4* (*Rondo*)
VAUXHALL NOVA	Prokofiev: *Peter and the Wolf*

VAUXHALL 1990	Khachaturian: *Spartacus* (*Adagio*)
WALLS CORNETTO	Di Capu: '*O sole mio*'
WATER PRIVATIZATION	Handel: *Water Music* (*Hornpipe*)
WOOLWICH BUILDING SOCIETY	Satie: *Trois Gnossiennes*
YARDLEY LACE PERFUME	Mozart: *Piano Concerto No. 21* (*Andante*)

Chapter Seven

What Music to Put on – and When

We all face the problem of what music to put on under different sets of circumstances – when guests are coming to dinner or when it is necessary (or, perhaps, helpful) to create the perfect romantic atmosphere. Psychologists tell us that the choice of music we select when showing prospective purchasers round our home can help sway them either way in their final decision.

Here follows a set of suggestions for what music it might be appropriate to put on and when. But, please, no responsibility can be accepted for plans that go wrong!

Waking Up

Baroque: Bach *Double Violin Concerto* and the *Suites for Orchestra*; Vivaldi *Concertos for Violin, Cello and Guitar*
Classical: Mozart *Concertos for Horn and Flute*; Haydn *Concertos for Violin and Cello*
Other: Prokofiev's *Classical Symphony*; Italian opera highlights

Cocktail-Parties

Baroque: Vivaldi concertos; Bach's *Brandenburg Concertos*
Classical: Mozart and Haydn string quartets
Romantic: Tchaikovsky and Dvořák *Serenades for Strings*

Afternoon Music

Classical: Mozart Divertimentos and Serenades; early Haydn symphonies
Romantic: Chopin Waltzes, Études and Mazurkas; Grieg *Piano Concerto*; Tchaikovsky orchestral music.

Dinner-Parties – Before

Baroque: Vivaldi concertos; Bach's *Brandenburg Concertos*; Bach's keyboard music, *Italian and French Suites*
Classical: Rossini and Donizetti opera highlights and overtures; early Mozart and Haydn symphonies; early Beethoven piano sonatas and concertos
Romantic: Chopin Waltzes and Mazurkas; Mendelssohn and Bruch *Violin Concertos*; Brahms *St Anthony Chorale Variations*
French: Debussy *Piano Preludes Books 1 and 2*; Debussy and Ravel *String Quartets*

Dinner-Parties – During

Baroque: Bach *Violin Concertos* and *Concerto for Oboe and Violin;* Handel's *Water Music;* Vivaldi *Concertos for Violins*
Classical: Mozart *Serenades* ('*Haffner*', *Eine Kleine Nachtmusik*); Mozart *Piano Concertos Nos. 19, 21, 23 and 27*; Beethoven *Serenade for Flute, Violin and Viola*; Schubert *String Quartets;* Tchaikovsky *Ballet Suites*

French: Debussy *Nocturnes* and *La Mer*; Ravel's *Introduction and Allegro*; Satie piano music; Fauré *Piano Quartets* and songs
Spanish: Villa Lobos, Granados, Albeniz guitar music
Italian: Rossini and Donizetti opera highlights; *Essential Pavarotti*; Kiri Te Kanawa, *Italian Opera Arias*
Others: Grieg's *Peer Gynt Suite* and *Piano Concerto;* Dvořák *Symphonies Nos. 5, 7 and 9*; Schumann *Piano Concerto*

Dinner-Parties – After

Classical: Slow movements from Mozart *Piano Concertos* and *Symphonies*; Mozart *Clarinet Quintet K.581*
Romantic: Brahms *String Sextets;* Mahler *Symphonies 1 and 4*; Rachmaninov *Piano Preludes* and *Piano Concertos*; Chopin *Nocturnes*

The *Romantic* Dinner-Party

Before: Spanish guitar music; Chopin *Piano Preludes;* Mendelssohn's *Songs without Words*; Schubert *String Quartets*
During: Tchaikovsky's *Serenade for Strings* and *Ballet Suites*; Rachmaninov's *Piano Concerto No. 3* and *Symphony No. 2*; Chopin *Ballades, Scherzos* and *Piano Concertos*; Liszt's *Consolations*; Schumann's *Piano Concerto in A minor*
After: Beethoven's *'Moonlight' Sonata* (1st movement); Rachmaninov *Piano Concerto No. 2*; Barber's *Adagio for Strings* and the *Violin Concerto* (*2nd movement*); Mozart's *Piano Concerto No. 21* (*2nd movement*); Beethoven's *Romances for Violin and Orchestra*; Chopin's *Nocturnes*; Tchaikovsky's *Romeo and Juliet*; Ravel's *Pavane pour une infante défunte*; Shostakovich's *Piano Concertos* (slow movements); Puccini opera highlights; Debussy's *Prélude à l'après-midi d'un faune*;

Bruch's *Violin Concerto* (2nd movement); Liszt's '*Un Sospiro*'; Debussy piano music; Ravel's *Bolero*

Relaxing

Slow movements from Bach's *Orchestral Suites* and *Solo Suites*; Handel's *Largo*; Mendelssohn and Bruch *Violin Concertos* (slow movements); Mozart's *Clarinet Concerto* and *Piano Concertos*; Chopin's *Piano Preludes*; Rachmaninov's *Piano Concerto No. 3*; Debussy *Nocturnes*; Ravel's *Daphnis and Chloé Ballet Suites 1 and 2*.

Chapter Eight

The Top Ten Performers

Over the last ten years there have been a handful of musicians who have captured the general public's imagination to the point that they have now become household names. These are performers who possess that rare combination of talent and charisma and who have benefited from having enormous media exposure which has all gone towards raising the profile of classical music and making it accessible to a much wider audience than ever before.

Sadly there are many other performers who are also outstanding but who have not yet received the high-profile attention that's been achieved by the artists mentioned here. I have included a recommended recording to introduce you to these artists if you don't already possess one.

Luciano Pavarotti

Perhaps responsible, more than any other, for popularizing classical music in the last few years, Pavarotti was featured in the 'Three Tenors' concert from Rome and sang '*Nessun dorma*' from *Turandot* by Puccini as the theme tune to the coverage of the World Cup from Italy in 1990.

Listen to: *Essential Pavarotti* (Decca 430 210–2)

Kiri Te Kanawa

The celebrated soprano from New Zealand who found international stardom after singing at the wedding of Prince Charles and Lady Diana Spencer.

Listen to: *Italian Opera Arias* (EMI CDC 7540622)

Nigel Kennedy

A highly talented violinist, originally from the Menuhin School, who has 'played' on the alternative image that he has created. He shot to fame in the late eighties and has broken all records with his very individual rendition of Vivaldi's *Four Seasons*.

Listen to: *Elgar Violin Concerto* (EMI CDC 7472102)

Placido Domingo

'The velvet voice in an iron physique' is how he has recently been described. He is a brilliant, versatile and energetic tenor who featured in the 'Three Tenors' concert from Rome in the summer of 1990 and has achieved fame at opera houses throughout the world.

Listen to: *The Best of Domingo* (Deutsche Grammophon – DG 415 366)

José Carreras

Featured in the 'Three Tenors' concert from Rome, Carreras has a lighter voice than the other two and displays a beautiful tender approach to his music-making. In the face of severe personal suffering he has maintained an active stance on the concert and operatic platform and is one of the world's best-loved singers.

Listen to: *Opera Arias* (Philips 416 248–1/4)

James Galway

Hailed as 'the man with the golden flute', Jimmy Galway made the flute extremely popular in the seventies and eighties. He has sustained the enthusiasm of the general public by his sparkling personality and sheer artistry and is among the most gifted wind-players that one is likely to hear.

Listen to: *Mozart Flute Concertos* (Eurodisc 610 130)

Yehudi Menuhin

Sir Yehudi Menuhin, OM, KBE, is one of the most remarkable musicians ever to have lived. Not only an exceptional violinist, but also a man of extraordinary human achievement who has inspired so much good work around the world.

Listen to: *The Young Menuhin* (Testament SBT 1003)

Georg Solti

A much admired conductor who has recently been featured in the Dudley Moore series entitled 'Orchestra'. Although the programme was not an overwhelming success, it did bring to the attention of the public at large this fine conductor who is perhaps at his best in the Romantic repertoire.

Listen to: *Tchaikovsky Symphony No. 6* (Decca 430 442–2)

John Williams

A guitarist of unique versatility who became well known for his work in the 'cross-over' field, performing a blend of jazz, rock and classical music with his band, Sky. Excellent, too, in the classical repertoire – a man of remarkable talent.

Listen to: *Spanish Music* (CBS DC 40140)

Julian Lloyd Webber

Brother of the celebrated composer of musicals Andrew Lloyd Webber, Julian is a cellist who has really caught the public's attention through the power of the media. He has made some fine recordings and has championed the cause of reaching the masses by also writing books.

Listen to: *Saint-Saëns Cello Concerto* (Philips 432 084)

Chapter Nine

The Historic Top Ten Performers

Over the last hundred years there have been a selection of artists that have been truly outstanding – performers who have shown the undisputed rare quality of genius. Listed here is my selection. Again, it is obviously my own personal choice, although I'm sure that few will disagree with the fact that these are all performers of exceptional talent.

For each artist I have also included a recommendation for a recording that would be well worth investigating if you are interested in hearing some of these great performers from the past.

Herbert von Karajan

Conductor of the Berlin Philharmonic Orchestra
Listen to: *Tchaikovsky: Six Symphonies* (Deutsche Grammophon – DG 429 675–2)

Maria Callas

Dramatic soprano

Listen to: *Mad Scenes and Bel Canto Arias* (HMV CDC 747283)

Jascha Heifetz

Virtuoso violinist

Listen to: *Sibelius, Prokofiev and Glazunov Violin Concertos* (RCA – RD 87019)

Sir Thomas Beecham

Conductor of the Royal Philharmonic Orchestra and the London Philharmonic Orchestra

Listen to: *Debussy*: '*Orchestral Works*' (EMI CD – EMX 9502)

Jacqueline du Pré

Virtuoso cellist

Listen to: *Elgar: Cello Concerto* (EMI CDC7 49911–2)

Sergei Rachmaninov

Virtuoso pianist and composer

Listen to: *Rachmaninov: Piano Concertos Nos. 2 & 3* (RCA RD 85997)

Dennis Brain

Virtuoso horn-player

Listen to: *Strauss: Concertos for Horn Nos. 1 & 2* (EMI CDC7 47834–2)

Vladimir Horowitz

Virtuoso pianist

Listen to: *At the Met* (Various) (RCA RCD 14585)

Enrico Caruso

Operatic tenor

Listen to: *The Complete Caruso* (Various) (RCA GD60495)

Glenn Gould

Pianist and musicologist

Listen to: *Bach: Goldberg Variations* (CBS CD37779)

Chapter Ten

Instruments of the Orchestra

The orchestra is divided into four families of instruments: strings, woodwind, brass and percussion.

String Instruments

String instruments all have stretched 'strings' (usually metal or gut) that vibrate to make the sound. They can be made to vibrate in three ways: by drawing a bow (a curved stick with stretched horsehair across it) over the string, by plucking the string with the fingers, or by a mechanical hammer hitting the string. The most common type of stringed instrument within the orchestra is the bowed type, and there are four important members of this family: violin, viola, cello and double bass.

Violin

Developed from earlier instruments, the viols, violins found their final identity shaped by the hands of master craftsmen in Italy in the seventeenth and eighteenth centuries. Three families of instrument-makers were particularly important in designing the violin as we know it today: the Amati, Stradivari and Guarneri families. Since that time no major changes have been introduced, and all other makers have based their own versions of the instrument on the basic designs of these Italian craftsmen.

In the right hands, violins can make the most beautiful sweet sound and the instrument is often used for tear-jerking melodies. When a collection of violins are playing the results can be most exhilarating. Listen to Tchaikovsky's *Serenade for Strings,* Vivaldi's *Four Seasons* or Mendelssohn's *Concerto in E minor* for beautiful examples of the different ways composers used the instrument in their compositions.

Viola

The viola is a slightly larger version of the violin and therefore projects a somewhat lower and darker sound. It is constructed in exactly the same way and, like the violin, is held under the chin on the left shoulder of the performer – the right hand being used to draw the bow across the strings.

Viola-players are for some reason the subject of cruel jokes among musicians, partly because in days gone by if you could not make a living as a violinist you could often move on to the viola and get away with a lot more. Generally the writing is not so flamboyant or demanding as that for the violin and viola-players can sometimes lurk anonymously among the middle-range textures of the orchestra.

On the other hand, in recent years we have seen the advent of the 'viola soloist' and quite rightly so, for the instrument can play with a beauty of tone and with almost the agility of the violin. Listen to *Harold in Italy* by Berlioz for a stunning example.

Cello

The word *cello* is short for *violoncello* and the instrument is the bass version of the violin. It, too, is constructed in much the same way as a violin; its four strings, however, are tuned exactly one octave lower than the viola. Because of its size, the cello is supported by a metal spike and is held between the knees of the player, who must obviously be in a sitting position.

The sound of the cello is unmistakable – rich, dark and warm – and for two beautiful examples listen to '*The Swan*' from *The Carnival of the Animals* by Saint-Saëns or the opening to Elgar's *Cello Concerto*. It can also be quite agile and a number of composers have exploited this in their work; Tchaikovsky wrote a lovely piece entitled *Variations on a Rococo Theme* for Cello and Orchestra. Following a most stately tune at the beginning are a set of variations of phenomenal technical difficulty. It really is a marvellous display and is well worth listening to.

Double Bass

This is the largest in the family of bowed string instruments and is so large and cumbersome that it is supported by a metal peg, with the player having either to stand or to perch on a stool in order to play the instrument comfortably.

The sound of the double bass is very deep and can be gruff, which is why it has largely remained an important member of the orchestra providing the bass line and is rarely heard in a solo capacity. The start of Schubert's '*Unfinished*' *Symphony* is an example of how well the double bass can project a lyrical melancholic theme, but I must also suggest that you listen to the Bottesini *Grand Duo for Violin and Double Bass*, which really demonstrates that in virtuoso hands the double bass can be an agile and exciting instrument.

★

Among the 'plucked' type of string instruments there are two that are commonly found within the orchestra: the harp and the harpsichord. Some will automatically say that a harpsichord is a 'keyboard instrument', and indeed it does have a keyboard, but remember that this activates the inner mechanism that actually plucks the strings within.

Harp

Often used in dreamy music, the harp has a beauty of sound that is quite unlike any other instrument and has been used to good effect in classical music, both in a solo capacity and as a member of the orchestra.

The player either plucks or gently strokes the fingers across the strings in order to make them vibrate and consequently produce the sound. There are all sorts of other subtle techniques to make different types of sound and these include lightly placing the palm of the hand on the middle of the string while plucking the upper half with the other hand – this produces what is called a harmonic, sounding mysterious and ethereal.

The harp has a set of seven pedals tuned to the scale of C flat, and the player can play in any key by using the pedals, adjusted by the feet. There are many examples of beautiful music played on the harp, my favourite being the *Introduction and Allegro* by the French composer Ravel. The piece is brilliantly written for the instrument, and in the right hands shows off many of the wonderful colours of sound that the harp can produce so beautifully.

Harpsichord

Forerunner of the modern piano, the harpsichord is altogether smaller in construction and has its strings plucked by small 'quills' or hard leathers. Most harpsichords only have a range of five octaves, and their sound is bright and brittle – perfect for cutting through the textures in Baroque string music, where they are frequently used to provide accompaniments.

Because of the stark clarity of the sound, harpsichords do sound extremely impressive in the contrapuntal music from the Baroque period and excellent examples are to be heard in the works of J. S. Bach.

Piano

The piano is another instrument that uses a keyboard to activate the mechanism required for setting the strings to vibrate. It does this by felt-covered hammers hitting the strings, which are stretched across a large soundboard. With the use of dampers (pedals to stop the sound) and the soft pedal which produces a more mellow and slightly muted sound, the piano has expressive capabilities far beyond that of the harpsichord and the forte piano that preceded it.

This led to the instrument being taken away from its former role as an accompanist within the orchestra as composers were inspired by the wonderful range of sounds that they could employ in their music. The solo repertoire for the piano developed rapidly. Occasionally the piano is used within the orchestra as part of the whole, but normally we now see the piano as a solo instrument in recital or providing the solo voice in a concerto with orchestra. Because of its flexibility it is also used to partner the voice and other instruments in songs, sonatas and chamber music.

Woodwind Instruments

Woodwind instruments rely on the vibration of air within a tube to make their sound and this can happen in two ways: by blowing across a hole in the tube (as on the flute) or by using a reed to vibrate at the top of the instrument (as on the oboe, clarinet and bassoon). As a rule of thumb, the longer the tube, the lower the pitch of the sound that will be produced; hence the tiny piccolo makes a shrill ear-piercing sound, while the long bassoon produces a more mellow, deeper tone.

Flute

The flute moved on from the recorder and is now made in the shape of a cylindrical tube (often of tin, silver or gold) and has a hole cut in the piece at the top known as the 'head joint'. It is held in a horizontal position by the player, who blows across the hole in the head to make the sound – rather like blowing across the top of a milk-bottle. To change the pitch of the notes on any wind instrument, the player covers or uncovers the holes down the tube. The greater the length of tube left vibrating, the lower the note.

The flute can have a pure sound with a pleasant 'breathy' quality to it and in the hands of an expert can be a highly agile instrument. Listen to the flute solo towards the end of the scherzo in Mendelssohn's *A Midsummer Night's Dream* for an excellent example, while the beginning of Debussy's *Prélude à l'après-midi d'un faune* provides a complete contrast, demonstrating the haunting evocative sound in a beautiful melody.

The piccolo is much shorter than the flute and is otherwise almost identical in construction. It sounds an octave higher and has a very bright piercing sound that many composers have found inspiring in orchestral works. Tchaikovsky's *Symphony No. 4* contains some excellent examples of piccolo writing, as do many overtures by Rossini.

Oboe

The oboe is made of wood and its tube is conical. The sound is made by the player vibrating a double reed that is inserted into the top of the instrument. This takes the form of someone making a sound blowing through two blades of grass held between the thumbs. On the oboe the two bits of shaved cane are held together by string to make what is called the reed; the player folds his lips around this reed and blows with some considerable effort!

The sound is somewhat nasal in character and has a rather mournful quality that has been used to good effect in the slow movement of Tchaikovsky's *Symphony No. 4*.

Also within the oboe family is the slightly longer and fuller-sounding cor anglais (English horn). It, too, has a double reed but differs by having a pear-shaped bell at the bottom of the instrument. The classic example of a piece for this instrument is that used on the Hovis commercial – the adagio from Dvořák's *Symphony No. 9* (*'New World'*).

Clarinet

Unlike the oboe and the cor anglais, the clarinet uses a single reed to vibrate and make the sound and this is held on to the mouthpiece at the top of the instrument. Clarinets are most often made of wood, but for beginners plastic ones are available. The sound and tone of the clarinet are extremely versatile; in some players' hands the sound can be beautiful and pure, ideal for lyrical classical music, while when played by others the instrument can assume a much harder, edgy sound, perfect for jazz or military band music.

Noted for its agility, many composers wrote fast and difficult music for the instrument, which has two other direct relatives within the family both of which are also found within the orchestra: the E flat clarinet and the bass clarinet. The E flat is the smallest of the family and is often likened to the piccolo. Listen to the solo in the *Symphonie fantastique* by Berlioz for a dazzling display of this instrument's sound and rather cheeky character. The bass clarinet is the deep, warm and mellow-sounding member of the woodwind section and is much larger than the ordinary clarinet; it has to rest on the floor with the player sitting down to play it comfortably.

Gershwin's *Rhapsody in Blue* opens with a stunning clarinet solo in a jazzy idiom, while the slow movement of Rachmaninov's *Symphony No. 2* is a beautiful example of the pure lyrical sound that can be produced on the instrument.

Bassoon

Another double-reed instrument, the bassoon is a long one that has to be bent in two to make it manageable. To some people's ears there is a rather humorous quality to the sound which has been exploited by a number of composers. However, like the cello in the string family, the bassoon can also be used with considerable agility, as Beethoven so clearly demonstrated when writing the last movement of his *Symphony No. 4*. Stravinsky, on the other hand, perfectly captured the haunting doleful nature of the instrument in the opening to his *Rite of Spring* ballet music; and, like the clarinet, the bassoon can be a remarkably versatile instrument.

It, too, has a bigger brother in the contra bassoon, the woodwind equivalent of the double bass, which produces an extraordinarily low and fruity sound.

Brass Instruments

By pursing the lips and vibrating them into a special mouthpiece one can make a sound on almost any of the instruments from the brass family, which all work on this basic principle. The sound of the individual members is very different, however, ranging from the French horn on the one hand to the piccolo trumpet on the other.

French Horn

This is a brass instrument made of a long conical tube that is wrapped round itself, ending in a large bell shape that points away from the audience. Early versions of the horn were just that – a length of tube – and the player was required to change the notes by simply varying the pressure of his lips on the mouthpiece. Needless to say, this was extremely difficult and placed severe limitations on the way that composers could write for the instrument. During the course of the nineteenth century a sophisticated valve mechanism was developed that enabled it to produce the complete chromatic scale by using varying lengths of tube at the will of the player, by pressing combinations of the three (or four) valves on the instrument.

The horn can produce all sorts of special effects and is one of the most versatile of all the brass family. By placing the hand in the bell of the instrument, the player can raise the pitch of the instrument slightly and it makes a curious muffled sound, while if a wooden mute is inserted into the bell the horn sounds 'distant'.

To hear examples of fantastic writing for the horn, listen to any of Mozart's *Horn Concertos* (the last movement of the 4th is the most famous) or the *Konzertstück* by Schumann for four horns and orchestra. In the orchestra, it seems that many composers chose this instrument when writing their most poignant and expressive melodies. Brahms' symphonies are littered with beautiful moments on the horn, while Richard Strauss was inspired to present the most heroic version of the theme from his symphonic poem *Don Juan* in a section for four horns.

Trumpet

The trumpet developed much like the horn from being an instrument with no valves to now having three to ease performance. It does differ, however, in that its tube is cylindrical and is played held directly in front of the performer's mouth. Originally only used for fanfare-like calls, the trumpet has since been used in all sorts of musical contexts. It is undoubtedly the most agile member of the brass family and tonally can play gently and quietly or at a hair-raising level if required.

Many composers have been inspired by its exciting sound and its use is also widespread in the jazz field. Composers like Gershwin in *An American in Paris* incorporated the jazzy sound of the instrument within the orchestra, while Beethoven, Tchaikovsky and Brahms used the trumpet in a more traditional way.

Trombone

The trombone looks entirely different from all the other brass instruments, having a slide that moves back and forth to alter the length of the tube. The instrument developed from the fifteenth-century sackbut and now is a familiar member of the brass section in the orchestra, as well as playing an important role in brass, military and jazz bands.

There are two main types of trombone: the tenor and bass instruments. The player has to gauge by 'feel' where the right place is for the slide and a considerable degree of skill is required, rather like that of violinists who have to put their fingers on the fingerboard by instinct in order to hit the correct notes.

Within the orchestra, trombones are most often used as part of the brass section as a whole and rarely have solos written for them. One of the most famous orchestral passages using a small group of trombones is in the overture *Tannhäuser* by Wagner.

Tuba

The largest and lowest-sounding instrument from the brass section is the tuba. It has a conical bore and a set of four or five valves that enable it to play a complete chromatic scale.

There are many different types of tuba: in Britain the military tuba or euphonium is well demonstrated in the famous solo within the piece '*Mars*' from Gustav Holst's suite *The Planets*, while the orchestral bass tuba is definitely at its best within the brass section as a whole. Listen to the arrangement by Elgar Howarth of Mussorgsky's *Pictures at an Exhibition* for an incredible display of all the instruments from the brass section, both as solo instruments and as members of the complete ensemble.

PERCUSSION INSTRUMENTS

The percussion instruments found in the orchestra have all developed from the oldest family of musical instruments, some still retaining their primitive form from the twelfth century and before.

There are three main types of percussion instrument: drums, tuned percussion and those with no definite pitch.

Drums

Of the drum family, the most commonly found within the orchestra are the kettle drums or timpani. These can be tuned to specific notes and take the form of a skin being stretched over a ring mounted on a basin-shaped shell. The pitch is changed by adjusting the tension of the skin, either with a foot pedal or with taps or keys that are placed around the top edge of the drum. The timpani are struck with sticks having padded ends.

The other drums often found in the orchestra are the bass and snare drums. The bass drum (the largest) has a narrow cylindrical wooden shell, covered at both ends with a skin and has a deep booming sound. A stick with a soft padded head is used to hit the drum. The snare drum also has a cylindrical shell but is much smaller. Over the bottom side are 'snares' (strings stretched across the skin) which rattle when the drum is struck. These can be lifted clear if a 'cleaner' sound is required. The snare drum is struck with a pair of hard thin wooden sticks.

Tuned Percussion

The glockenspiel and xylophone are often found in the percussion section. They are both constructed of a set of plates of definite pitch laid out over a frame that are struck by two small hammers. The plates of a glockenspiel are made of steel, while the xylophone's are made of wood and have a more mellow sound. In each case it is the construction of the frame that helps to add resonance to the notes produced.

Tubular bells are simply metal tubes of varying lengths hung on a large frame and struck with a wooden mallet. There are often eight which go to make the notes of a complete scale.

The celesta is rather like a toy piano to look at and has a set of metal plates attached to a wooden resonator. The sound is produced by a keyboard activating small hammers. The instrument was invented in the late nineteenth century and Tchaikovsky was so taken with the 'magical' quality of the sound that he featured it heavily in '*The Dance of the Sugar Plum Fairy*' in his *Nutcracker* ballet music.

Instruments with No Definite Pitch

There are literally hundreds of instruments that fall into this category, ranging from tambourines and castanets to instruments that emulate the sound of a horsewhip and a lion's roar!

Most commonly found within the orchestra are the tambourine (a wooden hoop, covered over at one end with a stretched skin and having small metal discs inserted into the hoop) which can make a variety of noises depending on the method of production – usually shaken or hit with the knuckles of one hand; the triangle (a steel rod bent to the shape of a triangle), which produces the characteristic 'ting' when hit with a small metal beater; cymbals (plates of brass, having leather handles), which can either be clashed together, rattled or struck with a drumstick; castanets (from Spain), which are two pieces of wood in the shape of shells and can either be held in the hand or shaken when attached to a stick; the gong (or tam tam), which is a large metal disc with a folded edge, suspended on a frame and struck with a soft-headed drumstick.

Other than going to a special demonstration of percussion instruments, the best way to hear them all in one go is to listen to Benjamin Britten's *Young Person's Guide to the Orchestra*, where a complete section of the piece is dedicated to nearly all of the instruments mentioned here. It is a remarkable noise and well worth hearing.

Index

Note: Bold figures indicate:
(i) main references to people who occur more than once
(ii) works on the CD/cassette